Gran Canaria Environment

Information Tourism

Author
Sam Kennedy

Copyright Notice

Copyright © 2017 Global Print Digital
All Rights Reserved

Digital Management Copyright Notice. This Title is not in public domain, it is copyrighted to the original author, and being published by **Global Print Digital**. No other means of reproducing this title is accepted, and none of its content is editable, neither right to commercialize it is accepted, except with the consent of the author or authorized distributor. You must purchase this Title from a vendor who's right is given to sell it, other sources of purchase are not accepted, and accountable for an action against. We are happy that you understood, and being guided by these terms as you proceed. Thank you

First Printing: 2017.

ISBN: 978-1-912483-45-7

Publisher: Global Print Digital.
Arlington Row, Bibury, Cirencester GL7 5ND
Gloucester
United Kingdom.
Website: www.homeworkoffer.com
.

Table of Content

Touristic Introduction 1
Culture 4
    Theatre & Music 6
    History 10
    Legend of San Borondon 29
    Legend of Atlantic 32
    Immigration to Louisiana 34
    Population 40
    Native Culture 43
    Learn Spanish 46
    Museum 49
Travel and Tourism 75
    Things to Do 75
    Attractions Gran Canaria 80
        Scuba in Gran Canaria 80
        Ride sand dunes on camelback 81
        Hike Caldera de Bandama 82
        Moonwalk at Roque Nublo 82
        Go stargazing 83
        Surf like a Big Kahuna 84
        Study ancient cave paintings 84
        Follow in Christopher Columbus's footsteps at Casa-Museo de Colón 85
        Sup Arucas rum 86
        Experience the Gran Canaria Carnival 86
        Have a grand day out in Palmitos Park 87
        Sip a cocktail on Playa de Las Canteras 87
        Get artsy at Museo Néstor 88
        Relax in the Viera y Clavijo Botanical Garden 88
        Chill out at Arguineguín 89
    Tour Recommendations 89
        Palmitos Park 89
        Cocodrilo Park 91
        Holiday World 92
        Mundo Aborigen 93
        Sioux City 95
        Cactualdea Parque 96
        Camel Safari 97
        Gokart 98

Jardín Botánico 98
Sport & Leisure *99*
  Air Sport..99
  Cycling 100
  Golf 101
  Rock Climbing 103
  Walking & Hiking 106
  Jet & Water Skiing 108
  Scuba Diving 109
  Surfing & Bodyboarding 110
  Windsurfing 110
  Sailing 111
  Big-Game Fishing 114
Shopping *117*
  Shoppingcentre 120
  Taxfree 135
  Markets 138
Service Area *143*
  Hotel Booking 143
  Baby - Services 145
  Weather 146
Accommodation *147*
  Apartments 147
  Bungalows 149
  Camping 150
  Villas 152
  Hostels 153
  Rural Hotels 154
  Private rentals 155
  Real Estate 157
Transport *157*
  Airport 157
  Bus 158
  Rent a Car 159
  Taxi 161
  Harbour 163
  Ferries 178
Gastronomy *179*
  Where to Eat 186
  What to drink 194
  Wine 201

Restaurant & Bar 211
   Nightlife 211
   Bars & Pubs 213
   Restaurants 215
Nature 217
   Beaches 217
   Fauna 229
   Flora 236
   Parks & Squares 247
Smoking 254
Hands-on Information 258
   Casino 258
   Electricity 261
   Police 261
   Post Offices 262
   Telephone 263
   Theft 264
   Tourist Office 266
   Water 267
   ESA - Space Agency 269
Holidays 271
   Christmas 271
   New Year 273
   Carnival 274
Immigration 275
   Moving 275
   Bank Account 277
   Gestoria 282
   Residencia / NIE 286
   Inspection Motorcars 290
   Insurance 291
   School 301

Touristic Introduction

The Canary Islands is a Group of Islands outside the African Northwest Coast. They consists of 7 Main Islands, divided in to Provinces:

- ➢ Las Palmas de Gran Canaria: Lancerote, Fuerteventura and Gran Canaria.
- ➢ Santa Cruz de Tenerife: La Palma, La Gomera, El Hierro and Tenerife.

The Canary Islands belong to Spain, and the Language is Spanish. The Inhabitants are Catholics, and are known for their honesty and Hospitality.

Gran Canaria is situated about 1.250 km from the Spanish Mainland. There are 83 km to Fuerteventura in the East, 62 km to Tenerife in the West, and 210 km to the Coast of Africa. All the Islands are Volcanic, and the oldest of the Islands, Lanzarote and Fuerteventura are about 30 million Years old. The youngest of the Islands, El Hierro, is only 750 thousand Years old. The area of the Islands is 7.447 km². The Population is 2.103.992(2009) Inhabitants, of which 838.397 (2009) lives on Gran Canaria.

> ➢ Furthermore we receive 8 9 million Tourists a Year.

On Gran Canaria you can have a very nice vacation, with much sun and bathing, and absolutely no stress. The Sun is almost guaranteed, you'll get excellent Food, lots of Pleasure, Shopping and many Sports Activities on Land on the Water. Beautiful Sand-Beaches, many exciting Restaurants, Well kept Golf-courses, Water sport Centres, Shopping Centres and delicious Seafronts.

Gran Canaria is the best known Island, but it is only the 3rd biggest, after Tenerife and Fuerteventura. It was on Gran Canaria the big Tourist Adventure began, first in Las Palmas, but later on most of the Tourism moved South to places, where the Sun could be counted on.

Tourism has taken over in the Neon lit Cities, bur frankly, The Island is pretty Beautiful, and when leaving Playa del Inglés and Puerto Rico behind, you'll find, that Gran Canaria is much more than the Tourist Cities by the Coast. Take a trip in the Mountains to the Idyllic Villages, with Palm Trees, tall Mountains, gigantic Pine Trees, Volcano Craters and Whitewashed Houses in Villages between Almond Trees.

Here Christmas Flowers and Bougainvilleas grow as big bushes, and Clematis climbs the Walls, and where Fig Cactus and Agaves stands side by side. Or you can take a Trip along the steep West Coast, or a Trip to the middle of the Island, 1949 m above Sea level.

If you have a 2 Week Vacation or more, it could be an adventure to visit one of the other Canary Islands, and Ferries and Planes are leaving to the other Islands on a daily basis from Las Palmas and Agaete. When leaving in the morning, it is possible to be back the same Day but you can find opportunities to stay the Night, direct from the Street. The smaller Islands are not so stamped by Tourists, so the possibilities of a different Vacation than you will find on one of the bigger Islands are great. Tickets to the other Islands are not expensive, so this type of Vacation is cheap.

Culture

The Canary Islands were incorporated into the Castilian crown during the 15th Century. From that time on Spanish traditions and culture have swept across the Islands.

A cultural tour round the islands is always worthwhile. The great cultural heritage has been carried over by every single inhabitant to the present time. You therefore find numerous traces of the native inhabitants of the whole area. In every village you can visit a church or chapel.

Gran Canaria boasts several interesting museums und culture centres, highlights of which are the recent Museo de la Ciencia y la Tecnologia (Science and Technology Museum) and the Casa de Colón (Christopher Columbus House) as well as the Centro Atlántico de Arte Moderno (Atlantic Centre of Modern Art) all of them situated in the city of Las Palmas.

Throughout the years, Gran Canaria has become a famous port of call for travellers. Visitors from all over the globe have come here and many have settled, bringing with them their own unique traditions and culture, transforming Gran Canaria into a truly cosmopolitan island.

Gran Canaria therefore is a mix of various different cultures. The society was always open to visitors from the seas and always welcoming towards new cultures. At the same time the locals, "Canarios", have always fought hard to maintain their own sense of identity and culture.

Nowadays Gran Canaria has a rich blend of artistic, archaeological and architectural heritage that come from a mixture of different races. There's not many other places on earth where you'll find such a wide variety of culture in such a small place.

The people of Gran Canaria love to celebrate and any excuse will do! There's always some kind of a festival or celebration going on, whether it's of religious, folkloristic or cultural nature, and there is always something going on somewhere on the island.

Many witnesses to the traditional handicrafts can also be found: basket makers, wrought-iron workers and tanners, to name but a few.

Traditionally the "Fiestas Patronales" are celebrated in the villages all year round. These are all civil-religious in character.

The processions which characterize these festivals are led by the local people in their traditional costumes. Also still evident today are the Apanados, the goats of the coastal region, which roam around free over the wide expanse of the local community.

At regular intervals they are rounded up by the herdsmen. An important part of this work is the Perro Majoprero, a native breed of dog which skilfully guards house and home.

In the meantime a firm place on the island's agenda, have the internationally renowned festivals such as the International Film Festival of Las Palmas, the Festival de Música de Canarias (Canaries Classic Music Festival) and the Festival de Ópera (Opera Festival).

Other events like the WOMAD (World of Music, Arts and Dance) or the Festival de Teatro y Danza de Las Palmas de Gran Canaria (Theatre and Dance Festival of Gran Canaria) bring still more influences of the international cultural panorama to this magnificent island.

Theatre & Music
Theatre and Music

Gran Canaria's cultural entertainment scene tends to be based around a variety of events in its festival calendar as opposed to featuring specific venues with ongoing musical or theatrical schedules.

Annual events involving opera, jazz, cinema, theatre and dance all feature in the calendar as well as a highly popular classical music event in the wintertime. Many of the big hotels and apartment complexes have live entertainment in the evenings featuring Spanish dancing and local musical acts.

Teatro Cuyás

Viera y Clavijo s/n

35002 Las Palmas de Gran Canaria

Tel. 928 43 21 80

Tel. 928 43 21 81 (Ticket reservations)

Fax. 928 43 21 82

Teatro Pérez Galdós

Plaza de Stagno 1

35002 Las Palmas de Gran Canaria

Tel. 928 43 38 05

Fax. 928 36 92 08

Recently re-opened after a long refurbishment, is the Pérez Galdós Theatre in Las Palmas. Named after the infamous Spanish Realist

Novelist, Benito Pérez Galdós, the theatre has under gone a massive face-lift, which included a controversial extension that cleverly combined the rich historical façade with minimalist modern architecture. A new stage and orchestra pit has also been added, which serves to improve the acoustics and provide the musicians with better visibility. The Pérez Galdós Theatre is at the heart of the Gran Canarian cultural scene and will host some of the best musical events on the island.

The theatre is situated in the Triana, district of Las Palmas, which is definitely worth visiting; here you can find many notable historical buildings as well as the main shopping street of this area. Visitors can look forward to a slice of true Canarian culture, discover cobbled streets overlooked by characteristic intricately carved wooden balconies, then take a seat in one of the pavement cafes, enjoy a 'café con leche' and watch the world go by.

Teatro Guiniguada
Mesa de León s/n
Las Palmas de Gran Canaria
Tel. 928 32 20 08
Fax. 928 31 63 43

Cicca

Alameda de Colón 1

Tel. 928 36 86 87

Auditorio Alfredo Kraus

Tomás Miller 49

35007 Las Palmas de Gran Canaria

Tel. 928 22 37 11 / 928 22 22 39

Fax. 928 26 26 96

Guided tours excursions in Spanish and English

Monday - Friday at 12.00 hour

The Concert House of the City also has lecture rooms. It is a beautiful modernistic building at one end of Las Canteras.
La Cicer. Ticket for the different arrangements is bought right here.

Auditorio de Teror

Orquesta Filarmónica
de Gran Canaria

Las Palmas has a extremely excellent and big Philharmonique Orchestra, which gives concerts in the theatre mostly on Fridays.

The Festival starts every year in the beginning of January, and continues until the last days of February. It takes place in the two capitals of the Archipelago, Las Palmas de Gran Canaria and Santa Cruz de Tenerife, where each and every one of the concerts is repeated. In addition to those, there is also a full concerts calendar on each of the smaller islands, Otros Escenarios (Other Venues).

History

History of Gran Canaria

The Canary Islands from Antiquity until now.
A few - it would appear very few - sea explorers reached the Canary Islands during ancient times. The islands lie in the Atlantic Ocean, into which very few sailors dared to venture. Furthermore, the ocean current called "Canaries Stream" flows in a south-westerly direction before veering to the west to sweep the unwary ocean vessel off to the Caribbean.

Centuries later, Europeans would make use of this current as a powerful aid in crossing the Ocean to reach America. (Christopher Columbus called in at Gran Canaria and La Gomera, and set sail from this island during his voyage of discovery in 1492. The Canaries were the last land sighted by the Spaniards before landing in the island of Guanahani -San Salvador- on October 12, 1492; and Canarian water and provisions supplied the "Pinta", the "Niña" and the "Santa María").

Those few Phoenicians, Greeks and Romans who reached the islands and managed to return home to tell their story, surrounded the Canaries in a mist of magic and legend. For centuries, even after the Spanish conquest, it was believed that the islands were the uppermost peaks of the lost continent of Atlantis of which Plato wrote.

Others identified them with the Elysian Fields, home to the blessed who knew no cold or pains. Similarly, the islands came to be identified with the Garden of Hesperydes, a paradise where golden apples grew under the guard of a gigantic flame-spewing monster (the Teide volcano?).

The Roman general Quintus Sertorius, whose ship was swept from Lusitania (Portugal) by a storm, speaks in the Its century BC of "some islands higher than Mount Atlas with a gentle climate". Plutarch called the Canaries "the Fortunate Islands", a nickname with they still bear and which has given rise to the term "Macaronesia" (the Happy Islands) to refer to the archipelagos of the Azores, Canaries, Madeira, and Cape Verde in the Atlantic.

Juba, king of Mauritania in Northern Africa and vassal of Rome in the Its century BC, sent an expedition out to explore the islands according to the writings of the famous naturalist Plinius.

The Guanches: The people from Tenerife.

Guanche was the name by which the natives of Tenerife called themselves. Guan Chenech meant "Man from Chenech", or man from Tenerife. With the passage of time, the term Guanche became identified with all the native peoples of the Canaries.

The first people living on the Canary Islands is veiled in mystery. The Guanches, had no recollection of the ways of the Sea; But at one time or other, they must have come across the Sea, if not to accept the theory, that they were descendants of survivors from the sunken Atlantis; a romantic but hardly scientific valid assertion.

The most recent investigations takes for granted, that there is a racial community between Guanches and Berbers, though there is doubt about when the Berbers came to the Islands. Berbers are not Arabic. They are Higher and fairer, and their past is for a great part veiled in mystery.

Kabyls have Berbic blood in them; Tuaregs are Berbers, and by the way the only people in the world, where it is the men and not the women, that are veiled from that the name.

They brought with them wheat and barley. They came from North Africa, originating from the same stock as the Berbers of the Atlas mountains. Yet this simple affirmation has caused - and still causes -

virtual rivers of ink to flow in polemical debate in which archaeology and ethnography become entangled in politics.

According to the tales of the European conquerors, the Guanches were a "highly beautiful white race, tall, muscular, and with a great many blondes amongst their numbers" Their great height must be understood in relation to the average height of Europeans at that time.

As for the presence of blondes, even today after many centuries of invasions and intermarriage, a heritage of blond hair and blue eyes is easily found among modern day Berbers of the Atlas region in Africa. There have of course been those who have tried to deny the Berber origins of the Guanches for political reasons, perhaps in order to avoid the possibility of potential territorial claims on the part of Morocco.

But this reasoning is totally illogical. The ancestors of the current Moroccan and Algerian Berbers who emigrated to the Canaries did so several centuries before the birth of Christ when neither Morocco nor Algeria nor their cultures yet existed.

The Guanches embalmed their dead after the same method, which was used by the Berbers, and maybe goes way back to the Egypt's. Modern Carbon 14 investigations have shown, that the oldest found mummies originates from about 200 years after Christ, and that there are anthropological common features with the Berbers. Furthermore the now extinct Guanche Language had a lot of Berberian words in it.

This same base was common to all the islands, but each island had developed into its own microcosm to the point where even the language had differentiated into distinct dialects. The islands were cut off one from the other as the natives did not know the art of navigation. They fished only in coastal tidal pools.

This is one of the great enigmas of the Guanches. How was it possible for a race of people to reach the shores of these tiny islands by sea, live surrounded by ocean with - on several islands - enormous forests of tall trees for raw material and yet ignore the sea, living as it were with their back turned to it?

Several possible answers to this mystery have been offered. Perhaps the people of the Canaries were simple shepherds who had been transported to the islands by a sailing people and later forgotten and left to fate. Other explanations might be found in the extraordinary difficulty of navigating the oceans surrounding the Canaries due to the strong currents flowing to the West and the trade winds blowing as strongly almost year round.

The names of the different islands and of their inhabitants (for those that are known) are as follows:

Tenerife

Chenech, Chinech or Achinech. It would seem that the natives of La Palma, seeing the snow-covered peak of the Teide on the horizon, called that island Ten-er-efez, "White Mountain" (from Ten, teno, dun, duna= mountain, and er-efez= white). Achenech was inhabited by the Guan Chenech, the men from Chenech.

The Guanches lived in a typically class society with 3, maybe 4 different rankings. The tribal Chief was on Tenerife called Mencey's (translated by the conquistadores to kings), and The Priesthood guañamer;

Fuerteventura
Maxorata, inhabited by the Majoreros or Maxos.

Lanzarote
Tyteroygatra.

Gran Canaria
Canaria, was inhabited by the Canarii or Canarios. On Gran Canaria existed a kind of double sovereignty with a king, guañarteme, his vassals, guavres and a high priest, a Fay can. Female prophets and oracle maker, often princesses, also had great power.

On Gran Canaria the all creator was called Alcorc. He was invisible, but could materialise in a rock, in a tree, and there as always some of his power in magic, in the sun.

La Palma
Benahoare, pronounced "Ben-Ajuar", and meaning "from the tribe of Ahoare" (tribe of the African Atlas). Island inhabited by the Auaritas.

La Gomera
Gomera, inhabited by the Gomeros.

El Hierro
Hero, inhabited by the Bimbaches. Aside the residents on El Hierro the Guanches believed in an mighty god, the all creator.

Gran Canaria
All the islands took their name from this one, because the Castilians started to call them 'Islands of Canaria', later 'Islas Canarias' (Canary Islands).

Gran Canaria is one of the Islands in the Canary group of Islands which consists of 13 Islands, of which only 7 is populated. With a surface of 1.562 km², Gran Canaria is the 3rd largest Island in the group, only surpassed by Tenerife and Fuerteventura.

All of Spain is divided in self-governing provinces, and the Canary Island is divided in two. An eastern province consisting of Gran

Canaria, Lanzarote and Fuerteventura, and a western province consisting of Tenerife, La Gomera, El Hierro and La Palma.

Gran Canaria is headquarter for the Eastern province and Tenerife for the Western. (The small Islands around the big Islands is named: Alegranza, Graciosa, Montana Clara, Roque del Este, Roque del Oeste and Isla de Lobos). The Islands are situated a little north of the Tropic of Cancer, namely between 28" and 29" n.br. which is on line with the South of USA in west and Egypt in the East. The Canary Island has a total area of 7.447 km².

From the Mainland Spain to Gran Canaria there are 1250 km., but from the Canarian East coast there are only 210 km. across the Atlantic Ocean to the African Continent. The mild Climate, that makes the quotation "The Islands of eternal spring" correct, even if it only goes for the southern coasts.

On the Northern coast it is often raining, and on the highest point of the Island, the temperature can be close to the freezing point at the same time there are 25 degrees on the south coast, a stretch of only 30 km. Just because of the big variations in the climate from north to south, Gran Canaria is often named as a mini-continent. Deciduous trees, cactus, tomatoes, papayas, pines coffee and bananas thrives fine in its own part of the Island.

To day the Canary Island has a population at about 1.968.280 Inhabitants, of which 802.247 lives on Gran Canaria, mainly occupied in tourism. The production of tomatoes and bananas is still playing an important role for the economy of the Island.

When the European Medieval Civilisation reached the Canaries, the Stone Age peoples language differed on the different Islands, but when They came from the same tribe, the population from all the islands were rapid to understand each other, when they, on the Spaniards ships, was brought from one island to another. But it looks like there was a certain difference in The looks. At Tenerife, earlier writers described the residents as blond, blue eyed and tall people, while the Gran Canarians was more brownish.

There was quite big differences in the life of the Guanches from island to island, but it is wrong to believe, that they only lived in caves. Subterranean constructions, which have been part of the habitations, exists near Telde and other places. The scanty furniture consisted of stools or stone blocks used as stools. Of the Goats, and in some islands the Sheep's coats, many necessities was produced, among others bags to contain the two most important things in the life of a Guanche; Water and Gofio. Weapon as we understand the word, the men didn't understand to produce. They didn't know how to use metal, and therefore was obliged to cut their weapons from stone and obsidian, or process the bones of the animals to arrowheads a/m.

Bows and Arrows they first learned about, when strangers invaded their islands. They used shaped rocks as missiles, and their tabonas was a combination of a long arrow or a small lance, with an point of flint, bone or tree. The heavier long spears was called magados. Their shepherd's crooks, añepaes, was used as weapon, and as a sign of dignity to the chieftains. They were much like crosiers.

The Guanche Was no noble savage, living under paradisal conditions. His food was very healthy and nutritious, and from the mummies it is known, that he reached a much higher average age than for instance his conquerors from Spain. The toasted corn, Gofio, which was grinded in a stone mill, was eaten as porridge or was baked to a kind of loaf. The Guanches was eating well and ample, no matter which place they had in society. On El Hierro, guatativos, enormous fiests, was held, and it wasn't unusual that an adult man ate a roasted kid and 20 rabbits. Afterwards he ate a dish of Gofio bread with goat butter and furthermore palm honey.

The Guanches lived in a typically class society with 3, maybe 4 different rankings. The tribal Chief was on Tenerife called Mencey's (translated by the conquistadores to kings), and The Priesthood guañamer; On Gran Canaria existed a kind of double sovereignty with a king, Guanarteme, his vassals, guavres and a high priest, a Fay can. Female prophets and oracle maker, often princesses, also had great power. Aside the residents on El Hierro the Guanches believed in an mighty god, the all creator, which on Gran Canaria was called Alcorc. He was invisible, but could materialise in a rock, in a tree, and there as always some of his power in magec, in the sun.

In Some places there was a matriarchal ruling; it was women governing. There are writers who thinks, that polyandry existed on the islands, and that noble woman often had more than 1 husband. On Gran Canaria and possibly also on other islands was in force for the kings, that they had jus primæ noctis; that is, that the lord of the area had a sexual first right to all virgins, who wanted to get married. And he could delegate this right, to whom he wanted. Below the nobility (on Tenerife achimencey) was the peasants (achicaxna) and the servants (cichiciquitzan), who were counted no more than slaves.

But there was one more caste below them, these pariahs who were embalming the dead. On La Palma the Island a human being who felt death nearing, said farewell to his family, with the words: vako guare- "I want the death to come". Those closest to him followed him to the cave of death, where his bed was made, before a big stone was placed in front of the opening of the cave. About a week thereafter the cave was opened, and the body of the dead was given to the embalmer. On Gran Canaria it was the Fay can, who like the rest of the nobility had a long beard and a long hair, who made the initiation.

The probationer, who was permitted to let his hair grow, so it was well past his shoulders, stepped in front of the sábor´en (the council), and the Fay can asked in high voice, if any of those present had seen this young man sneak in between the goats of other people to steal an animal or to milk it, if anyone had seen him being improper towards a high-born lady … she was so respected, that it was considered a resentment to talk to her, or to get near her, when she was alone. If the assembly denied this, the Fay can cut off the hair of the young Esquire right below the ears and gave him a magado, a worriers lance. With this he should, in times of war, serve his master and king. And thereby he was admitted in the nobility. But could someone prove, that the probationer had addressed a high-born woman while she was alone, or was milking a goat which wasn't his, all his hair was cut off and he had to live the rest of his life as a slave.

A low-caste woman could make a career for herself by marrying, because by marrying she received the same place in society as her husband. The ways of marriage was very different from island to island. Om Lanzarote the women often had 3 husbands and got the rank of the husband with the highest rank. It could cause some differences by the noble husband, because the one of the 3 who had enjoyed the matrimonial rights by the wife in common in a month, the next month had to serve as her valet also the nobleman.

The 3rd month however he was left to himself. And no woman could marry unless she had been on a fattening diet. When arrangements about marriage had been made and a kind of betrothal had taken place, the young woman, in a whole month, went to bed and during that time let herself be waited on with all kinds of delicacies; goat fat mixed with honey, lamb in cream and delicious Gofio-cakes en crouted with dates, everything in the hope to become so fat and thereby so attractive as possible. It is estimated that new-married Guanche women weighed about 120 kilos.

The groom had a right to repudiate his wife to be, if he even after the fattening diet found her to skinny. Normally there was a prohibition against marriage between closely related, but chiefs and noble priests could obtain a exemption at the sábor'en and marry their sisters, as was usual in prehistoric Egypt. On the Gomera the Guanche men offered their wives to noble guests but they kept an open eye on, which children was born as a result of these visits.

There was often war between the different small kingdoms (or chieftain areas)on The Canary Islands. Only the people on El Hierro was thought to have lived peaceful lives because it was ruled by a king, that loved peace and hated bloodshed. On the second largest island in the group, Fuerteventura, there were two kingdoms Xandia towards south and Maxorata towards north who constantly was in war with each other, the one part build a wall across the island. Also Gran Canaria had two kingdoms who, however until the Spanish conquering, was gathered under one common king.

The reasons for war was often an argument about earth, or cattle who had strayed into the land of the other state. But relationship feuds, who could come from jealousy, or be so old rooted, that everybody had forgotten the originate cause, now and then brought along fights between the chief areas. The wars doesn't seem to have demanded many deaths. As in fights, playing in peacetime often started with single combat. Two men from either side placed themselves in front of each other in about 50 meters distance, and each armed with about 20 round stones, placed on the earth before them.

One of them started the fight by taking a stone and throw it after his opponent. For him, he had to avoid being hit or catch the stone and throw it back against his opponent. There after the opponents moved closer to each other, and when there were 8 paces between them, the test really started. He, who without moving his left foot could avoid the stone or catch it and throw it back was the winner. It so happened that the chiefs ended the war by shouting Gama Gama, and if the people shouted the same, which means: " enough", one sat down in peace and negotiated the dispute.

One thing should be written with capital letters about the Guanches; they knew enough about sudden assaults and guerrilla wars, but they never tormented a defeated enemy. Torture was unknown to them, and when the inquisition came to the islands, the Guanches at first didn't understand, that people could be so wretched in the name of religion. To them God was a very airy thing plateistisk the religious historic would name it a being which was everywhere in nature, and had to exterminate now and then, but to whom torture was an abomination.

The aboriginal population of the Canary Islands, the Guanches, had a special care for a type of demanding wrestling, where "fair play" was in the seat of honour. They called it "La Loch Canaria" and met regularly to tournaments in front of an enthusiastic public to national festivals, official gatherings and arrangements. Even to day you can see this Canarian fighting sport.

The central parts of the island are dominated by a big and very hilly mountain landscape, created by thousands of volcanic eruptions during 16 million years. The last eruption on the island was in the area Bandama, about 2000 years ago. On the north side of the island, exposed to the humidity of the trade winds, you experience vigorous canyons, in contrast to the bush steppes and half deserts of the south coast.

The most important source of income on Gran Canaria has varied through the years: After sugar production came wine growing, and then the natural colours from the Cochenille lice, then tomatoes, potatoes and bananas. For the time being the tourism is the most important followed by fishing which also gives with a big part of the income for the island. Because if there is something which has been good to the common mans living, not only on the Canary Islands, but also in Spain, and by that have made him self-conscious, it is tourism, which is the most important way of income in Spain.

And there is no country in the world, where this development as a whole hasn't hurt the single citizen , in Spain and special on the

Canary Islands, where the residents are surrounded by thousands of tourists and still have kept their origin, their honesty and their pride.

It doesn't matter which government there is in Spain, the Canarian people and the tone they use among themselves much more democratic, then we find it even in Scandinavia. .

Important Years in the History of Gran Canaria:

2500 BC.:	Earliest sign of people on the islands.
Ca. 1100 BC.:	Cartago's and Phoenicians Discover the Canary Islands.
800 B.C.:	The Canary Islands was discovered by Homer the Greek.
82 year BC.:	The Romans surely sailed to the Canary Islands. It was them who named the Canary Islands (Dog Islands) else they only called them "The Happy Islands".
23-79 AC.:	Plinius den older Describes in his "Encyclopedia Naturalis Historia" a group of Islands. One of these islands he calls "Canaria".
999:	Some Arabs came to the islands and built a peaceful colony.
11-1200:	Arabian sailors arrives on the islands in the 11 hundreds.
1334:	French ships visits the islands.

Gran Canaria Environment

1340:	Spanish and Portuguese ships are making the first slave cruises to the islands.
1344:	Pope Clemens VI named the Spanish nobleman Luis de la Cerda a king of the Canary Islands.
1382:	Spaniards settled peacefully on the Island, but there was a fight with the Guanches, where they murdered all the Spaniards.
1394-1460:	Prince Henrik, the Portuguese sailor are making several expeditions to Gran Canaria, but without luck.
1478:	One of queen Isabella of Spain's officers, Juan Rejón lands on the north coast of Gran Canaria the 24. July, with more then 600 men armed with guns. With this landing the city of Las Palmas was founded. They were met with strong resistance from the residents of the islands.
1479:	Alcácovas-agreement decided, that Spain has a right to the Canary Islands where after they sent Juan Rejón, Pedro de Vera and Alonzo de Lugo to conquer them. The Guanches who where left behind didn't want to end like slaves, or second class people, so they hurried to arrange marriage between their young girls and Spanish soldiers. By this move the Guanches got French blood in their veins.
1483:	After long, hard fights Juan Rejón won over the islands guanartemer (kings) Thenesor Semidan in Gáldar og Doramas I Telde governing the two realms on Gran Canaria.
1492:	Christopher Columbus stops on Gran Canaria and La Gomera in his way to America.
1493:	Spaniards overcomes the Canarian resistance.
1522:	The Frenchman Jean Fleury attacks Las Palmas. He is beaten.
1537:	The king of Spain forbid slavery.

1599:	Here the Dutchman van der Does succeeded in conquering Las Palmas who came to pay severe taxes.
1657:	England tries in vane to conquer the islands.
1670:	The Dutch fails in an attempt to conquer the Island.
1796:	England attacked under command of Lord Horace Nelson the island Tenerife. By this famous battle he lost his right arm. Spain and France joined forces to prevent the English in conquering the islands.
1799:	The German geographer and natural scientist Alexander von Humboldt lands on the island on his trip to South America.
1820:	Las Palmas becomes the official capital of Gran Canaria.
1852:	Queen Isabel II gives the Canary Islands status as a free trade area and even to day they enjoy special trade arrangements inside the EU.
1888:	Steam Post boats sails between the Islands.
1906:	Alfonso XII is the first Spanish monarch to visit Gran Canaria.
1912:	Self-government is introduced (Cabildo Insulares).
1927:	The Canary Islands are divided in two provinces: Las Palmas de Gran Canaria and Santa Cruz de Tenerife.
1930-31:	The airport is built.
1935:	Franco is appointed Chief of Staff, but when a peoples government is taking over power in Spain, he is made governor on the Canary Islands. Here is the preparations to the Spanish Civil War (1936-39) made.

1945:	The private air travel is growing strongly and tourist money is background for the economical development on the Islands.
1950-1970:	The tourism on the islands began. Tourism is to day the biggest trade on the islands.
1975:	General Franco dies ob the 20. November, And the day after Juan Carlos is appointed king of Spain and a new chapter in Spain's History begins. Spain is developing to a modern democracy.
1982:	The Canary Islands receives Self-government, controlled from Madrid.
1986:	Spain joins the EU. The Canary Islands receive a special status.
1993:	Dedication of the new Airport.
1997:	New visiting record on the Canary Islands with 8 million tourists a year.
2000:	The Canary Islands receives about 12 million tourists 2 millions of these comes from the Spain mainland.
2002:	The EURO is introduced as mean of payment on January the 1.

Legend of San Borondon

The Ghost Island: San Borondon (Saint Brendan)

The legend of San Borondon

Is there an eighth Canary Island?

While living or holidaying in the Canaries have you heard the stories about the lost city of Atlantis being somewhere around here?

The Canaries are seven islands... but an eight isle is still searched! It is the ghost island, the mysterious one, the island of San Borondón. San Borondon is the Canarian name of *St. Brendan* from Clonfert (480-576). He was an Irish monk who played the leading role in one of the most famous legends of Celtic culture. He went on a journey to the promised holy land, the island of happiness and wealth.

The Irish poem tells that Brendan was a monk of Tralee, County Kerry. He was ordained priest in the year 512 AC. He sailed with 14 other monks in an old and fragile boat which went far away in the Atlantic Ocean.

Other accounts tell of an attack on Brendan's boat by monsters or island inhabitants: "pelted with flaming, foul smelling rocks". The voyagers' account reaching the very edge of Hell itself, with great fiery furnaces, with rivers of gold fire an erupting volcano to an uninformed eye could look very similar.

They landed on an island where they found trees and other kinds of vegetation. They held a mass and suddenly the island started sailing. It turned into a gigantic sea monster, and they were on top of his back. After many similar events they returned to Ireland.

During the conquest of the Canary Islands in the 1400's, there were many stories about an 8th island that could sometimes be seen west of La Palma, La Gomera and El Hierro. But when the sailors tried to reach the island it got covered with mist and disappeared.

This island got associated with the island St. Brendan found, and was therefore called *San Borondon* by the Canarians. People believed firmly in its existence, and there were even detailed accounts from an odd sailor or two who swore that they had landed on the island and explored it before the land had sunk again into the Ocean. In some international treaties signed by the Kingdom of Castille it was stated, concerning the Canary Islands, the Castilian sovereignty over "the islands of Canaria, already discovered or to be discovered"; just in case...

You can even find old maps of the island in Museo Canario, located in Las Palmas, the capitol of Gran Canaria. This legend is very much alive, still today. And don't be surprised if you talk to some old fishermen who will tell you stories about people who have seen this island...

The island was called "Aprositus", the Inaccessible, and in other versions of the legend is named "Antilia" or "Island of the Seven Cities", cities which were supposed to have been founded by seven legendary bishops.

The archives of the 18th century inform about official inquiries by the authorities of El Hierro, where tens of witnesses declared having seen the bewitched island from the summits of El Hierro's mountains. An expedition in search of the island sailed from Santa Cruz de Tenerife as a result of this inquiry.

The persistence of this legend in the islands' folklore is amazing. San Borondón is still alive in the islands' people imagination. There is probably no one islander of Tenerife, La Palma, La Gomera or El Hierro who sometime has not looked from the mountains of his island into the sea, searching the lost island of San Borondón in the western horizon where the sun sinks in the cobalt-blue waters of the Atlantic Ocean.

Many base on this legend the affirmation that Irish sailors reached possibly in the High Middle Ages the shores of North America or Newfoundland, Iceland and other Atlantic isles.

Legend of Atlantic

The legend of Atlantis is one of the most fascinating mysteries of the world. Did it exist or was it simply a myth?

If it did exist where on earth was it and where did it go?. Is The Canary Islands the uppermost peaks of Atlantis mountains?. Whether you believe there is any truth in the legend is irrelevant as the story itself is so fascinating.

The descriptions of Atlantis as a paradise with fertile soils and a wealth of water has also brought for some the legend to the Canary Islands, which have long been associated with an abundance of agricultural produce. The Canary Islands are often referred to as a paradise in miniature. Blessed with beautiful year round temperatures and lands that are one minute dry barren deserts and at the next turn thick green forests or volcanic as far as the eye can see and it is easy to see why so many link Atlantis with the Canaries.

Atlantis is the name of an island first mentioned and described by the classical Greek philosopher Plato. According to him this island, lying "beyond the pillars of Hercules", was a naval power, having conquered many parts of western Europe and Africa. Soon after a failed invasion of Athens, Atlantis sank in the waves "in a single day and night of misfortune" due to a natural catastrophe which happened 9,000 years before Plato's time.

As a story embedded in Plato's dialogues, Atlantis is mostly seen as a myth created by Plato to back up a previously invented theory with real facts. Some scholars express the opinion that Plato intended to tell real history. Although the function of the story of Atlantis seems to be clear to most scholars, they dispute whether and how much Plato's account was inspired by older traditions. Some scholars argue Plato drew upon memories of past events such as the Thera eruption or the Trojan War, while others insist that he took inspiration of contemporary events like the destruction of Helike in 373 BC or the failed Athenian invasion of Sicily in 415-413 BC.

The possible existence of Atlantis was actively discussed throughout the classical antiquity, but it was usually rejected and occasionally parodied. While basically unknown during the Middle Ages, the story of Atlantis was rediscovered by Humanists at the very beginning of modern times. Plato's description inspired the utopian works of several Renaissance writers, like Francis Bacon's "New Atlantis". More than ever, Atlantis inspires today's literature, from science fiction to comic books and movies.

Immigration to Louisiana

The Canary Islanders of Louisiana

The archipelago of the Canaries consists of seven main islands, having a total area of less than 6 percent of the size of Louisiana, lying about sixty-five miles west of Morocco in Northern Africa. They were formed as a result of volcanic activity. It is a rugged, mountainous terrain, and plains are almost nonexistent. Lack of water is a serious problem. The westernmost islands receive the most rain, while the two islands closest to the Sahara Desert and lower in elevation have some deserts.

The higher elevations on some of the western islands have pleasant temperatures, and crops of wheat, barley, potatoes, dates, chestnuts, bananas, sugarcane and other subtropical plants can be grown.

The ancient natives of the Canary Islands were the Guanches, who lived in a Stone Age way of life. The language is related to the ancient idioms of North Africa, but has disappeared except for a few words. The Guanches never developed writing and did not know the use of boats in the fifteenth century. They lived a pastoral life, caring for their goats, sheep, and pigs. Some of them lived in huts, but the majority lived in caves. Adults dressed in skins or grasses sewn together, while the younger people went about naked. They developed a system of government that included judges, laws, and kings. The Gaunche weapons were mainly sticks, spears, and stones. Their religion consisted of belief in a single god, and they carefully buried their dead after embalming the bodies.

The origin of the Guanches has mystified scholars. The earliest Gaunche inhabitants have been described as robust, fair skinned, and handsome. Recent studies classify the people into two groups called Cro-Magnon and Mediterranean. The Cro-Magnon type is described as broad-faced, robust, long headed and fairer than the Mediterranean type. The Mediterranean type is described as long faced, delicate, and having a short, broad skull. Evidence points to Northwest Africa as the origination point for the Gaunches, sometime between 2500 and 1000 BC.

Stories about the Canaries circulated around the Mediterranean before the times of the Romans. King Juba II of Mauretania who reigned between 25BC and AD 25 sent an expedition to investigate the islands. They found no human but encountered ferocious dogs. King Juba named the islands for the dogs, canine in Latin being canaria. The well-known songbirds derive their name from the islands rather than giving it to them.

After the collapse of the Roman era, the islands disappeared from recorded history for nearly a thousand year. The Genoese arrived in 1291, followed by the Portuguese in 1341, and the Majorcans in 1342. Beginning in the fourteenth century, the Europeans often sacked and enslaved the natives. Gaunches were sold as slaves before 1400 in Seville and Valencia and though the fifteenth century. The Spanish crown of Fernando and Isabella finally defeated the remaining Gaunches and the Canaries came under Spanish control. Spanish names, religion, and customs were forced upon the Gaunche. Spanish nobles seized the best agricultural lands, treating the Gaunches in the most barbaric manner, coercing them into serfdom. Economic conditions deteriorated. The native tenant farmers and their families were starving.

War erupted in the English colonies of North America in 1776. Spain's vast Louisiana colony in 1763 had only approximately eleven thousand people, less than half of whom were white. England seized several Spanish boats on Lake Ponchartrain in May 1777. In August 1777, the Spanish Crown commanded the governor and commandant general of the Canary Islands to enlist seven hundred men for service in Louisiana. Emigration to Louisiana offered to the islanders opportunity to escape the deplorable conditions in which they lived. More than three hundred inhabitants of Gomera chose to leave for Louisiana. The recruits appear to have come from five of the seven islands: Hierro and Fuertenventura yielded no volunteers.

The immigrant soldiers needed to be between 17 and 36 years of age, at least five feet one-half inch tall, robust and without noticeable imperfections or vice. Preference was given to married men. The wives, children, and close relatives of the recruits would be transported to Louisiana at royal expense. Eight ships transported the 2,010 Islenos from the Canaries. The last ship, El Sagrado Corazon de Jesus, departed on May 31, 1779, but was detained in Havana because the Governor of Havana did not think Louisiana was a safe place due to proximity of the British troops at Baton Rouge. Many of these Islenos never finished the journey to Louisiana. Copies of the passenger lists of the eight ships are in the books referenced.

Louisiana Governor Bernardo de Galvez welcomed the first group of Canary Islanders in November 1778. He decided to employ all the immigrant-recruits as settlers only, because of the impossibility of keeping the married recruits in the regiments with their large families. He established the first community, Valenzuela, on Bayou Lafourche, just past Donaldsonville. Today, this is the site of Belle Alliance plantation, and there is an historical marker marking this site as Valenzuela. Galveztown was established on the banks of Bayou Manchac where it joins the Amite River, and as a buffer to the British who controlled the area north of Bayou Manchac. Barataria was established on the west side of the Mississippi River below New Orleans and Terre-aux Boeufs on the east bank. The settlements at Galvez and Barataria both failed because of continuous flooding. The Islenos in St. Bernard parish quickly adapted to the area and increased their income by fishing and trapping in addition to farming. The Islenos in Ascension and Assumption parishes settled down to farming, the main crop being sugar cane. Many Canary Islanders' descendants today still live in the Bayou Lafourche and St. Bernard areas.

The land grants were supposed to consist of approximately three arpents of bayou front (576 feet) by 40 deep (7,680 feet), but the grants were irregular in size, due to the curving of the bayou. The government supplied them well, sometimes lavishly. Some of them received a cart and two horses valued at 125 pesos. One example, a family numbering seven persons received: 150 ounces of cloth, 30 ounces of printed linen, 4 hats, 10 plain and 4 silk handkerchiefs, 6 pairs of stockings, 16 ounces of cloth of white thread, 4 needle cases, 8 thimbles, 1,000 pins and needles, 3 fusils (flintlocks), 3 pounds of gunpowder, 4 shaving razors, 5 axes, 8 hoes, 2 shovels, 10 ounces of Limburg cloth, 2 1/2 pesos in coin per person, 20 pesos for the purchase of a mare, and a number of other items. The government built the colonists at Galvez wooden houses, 16 x 32 feet, with a gallery on one side.

Sugar cane was brought from the Canary Islands and introduced into Louisiana agriculture. Canary Illanders have labored in the sugar industry continuously and have had a large part in making the industry the success it is today.

Islenos have distinguished themselves in the War of 1812, Civil War, and WWI and WWII. Although, many remained clannish and aloof from outsiders until the early 1900's, most have since valued education and many have served honorably in governmental positions. All Isleno descendants should be proud of their unique heritage.

Population

The Gran Canaria Population

The people of Gran Canaria are known for their hospitality to visitors and their peaceful and kind natures. Being so by reason of the continuous passage of peoples and cultures that has occurred as a result of the island's strategic position between three continents.

The island's famed spring weather throughout the year and its natural resources provide the inhabitants of Gran Canaria with a very high quality of life.

Almost 96 per cent of the inhabitants of the Canary Islands are Roman Catholics, who are very tradition-conscious, which can be witnessed on big religious feast days and particularly during the 'Semana Santa' (Holy Week before Easter), when extensive celebrations take place all over the islands.

Gran Canaria is the most populated island of the Canarian Archipelago, (802.247 inhabitants in the year 2005), and is located near the West

African Coast. Its population is Caucasian, from Spanish, Portuguese and French origins.

The population of Gran Canaria is young in comparison with that of the rest of the country and Europe, given the fact that the largest part of the population is between the ages of 15 and 45 years, the growth rate of the population being 3.71%, compared with the national average of 0.27%.

Maybe because of its youth, it is also the most cosmopolitan of the islands (especially the capital, being home to almost half of the population), which is what lends so many special traits to the island, finding expression in its open nature and cultural diversity.

A facet of the inhabitants that always intrigues the visitor is their manner of speech, which, despite the fact that it falls within the confines of perfectly understandable Spanish, has also been influenced by the linguistic diversity that was brought to the islands by the continuous passage of foreign visitors through the course of time.

For many people, the speech of the people of Gran Canaria is reminiscent of the Latin American dialects, in the sense that both have a sweetness of intonation, while it is also replete with curious practices, such as the use of the affectionate diminutive (Antoñito instead of Antonio) and the substitution of the "c" and "z" by the "s".

In any event, the people of Gran Canaria are very accustomed to foreign languages and one can easily find local inhabitants who have taught themselves to speak and understand many foreign languages.

The island has a population of 802.247 with 378.628 (year 2005) of those in the capital city of Las Palmas de Gran Canaria. Las Palmas de Gran Canaria is also the capital of the province of Las Palmas, (Gran Canaria, Fuerteventura and Lanzarote) and also one of the two capitals of the autonomous community of the Canary Islands, along Santa Cruz de Tenerife.

Although smaller than Tenerife and Fuerteventura, Gran Canaria houses more than half of the entire population of the archipelago, mostly in Las Palmas. It's now Spain's seventh-largest city.

The Gran Canaria of today boasts, with an average of 465 people per square kilometre, the highest housing density not only of the archipelago but also of all European regions. Almost half of its population concentrates in the city of Las Palmas, a great ethnic mix lending it a very cosmopolitan image.

As a result of having been a bridge between Europe and the continents of America and Africa for so long, many members of other nations in particular merchant families and seafaring people have settled on the Canary Islands from early on.

Their descendants are fully integrated in the island's society, where nobody would deny them their status of a genuine 'Canario'

Native Culture

Native Culture in Gran Canaria
We know about the native Gran Canarian culture from written accounts, oral traditions, and more and more archaeology. Many sites give evidence of an agrarian culture with a religious system based on fertility rites.

Finds such as complex burials and organized food storage and distribution systems reveal a well-developed hierarchical society. As more study is made of the island's archaeological remains, Gran Canarias past continues to unfold.

The origin of the first dwellers of the Canary Islands was in Northern Africa and presents natural and various contrasts with the later level of economic and social development.

During the 15th century the Spanish Crown wrested control of the Canary Islands from the Berber-speaking natives. Over the succeeding centuries the islands have been Europeanised to such an extent that the average visitor might think that all trace of the pre-Spanish culture had been lost long ago.

This, however, is far from being the case, as the Canary Islanders still maintain many aspects of the native culture, particularly in the countryside and in the smaller islands where the effects of the tourist boom have been less felt. .

The original inhabitants of Gran Canaria based their economy on agriculture more than on cattle, harvesting, gathering of seafood or fishing.

Barley was the product par excellence in the diet of the first settlers of the island, and with it they elaborated gofio (toasted and ground cereal meal), with which they took wheat and beans. A distinct characteristic that still remains in Gran Canaria are the silos, which were places in caves where the original inhabitants kept their products.

Natives stayed mainly in big settlements of semi-urban structure. The highest concentration of the population was centred in Gáldar, Telde or Arguineguín.

Caves served as lodges, a tradition that still exists in Gran Canaria. The other type of housing the natives used was excavated in the ground - which had a round shape on the outside- and made of big blocks of dry rock and a wooden cover.

Hierarchy was crucial in the social structure of the native communities in Gran Canaria. Firstly, there were the nobles, with hereditary titles and power of decision in political administration and economy, on top of being the land and cattle owners, and the villains, to whom the class directly above gave plots of land and good cattle in exchange for their payment in kinds and services.

The Guanarteme, absolute leader of the native community, shared his power with the Faycan, the figure second in importance in the native community of Gran Canaria and on whom fell the weight of religious rituals and services. Nevertheless, this figure was not exempt from playing political, military or social roles.

Acorán was the supreme god of the Grand Canaries, to whom the natives offered their sacrifices and offerings. The Harimaguada was the feminine figure of nobility who was preserved from her childhood to share the same labours as the Faycan.

Gran Canaria boasts the greatest repository of native art and culture of all the islands in the archipelago. Some of the most outstanding archaeological finds consist of cave paintings, such as the ones in the painted cave ("Cueva Pintada") of Gáldar, which is decorated with geometric motifs that are made up of squares, triangles and circles, all painted in red, ochre and white.

The natives had a great reputation as artisans, whose techniques and means reach our days. Mud was one of their main raw materials. Apart from domestic utensils and icons, such as the Ídolo de Tara, the natives made Masonry, knives, woodwork or spinning became, with time, part of the long list of handicrafts that are nowadays a legacy maintained or recovered by the current population of Gran Canaria.

These motifs -which are similar to the ones that have been found on ceramics and 'pintaderas' (clay seals)- are found throughout the arts and crafts of Gran Canaria.

The island territory has a wealth of stone quarries, which the people of Gran Canaria have used for a host of applications, including the building of roads, bridges, benches, mills, troughs and fountains.

The use of caves as dwellings and not only as a storehouse for agricultural tools or as a stable is still a constant in the Canary Islands, an aboriginal cultural heritage that was well versed in the advantages of digging rooms in the depths of the mountains when the surrounding environment was favourable.

Learn Spanish

Learning a foreign language is a challenge for everyone. However, if you want to live in Spain it is important to be able to communicate in

Spanish. That will help you get the most out of your life there. Check out our information about language courses and schools.

Learning Spanish

How to learn the language

Learning a language is a challenge for everyone, but if you want to live in a foreign country, it is very important. As for any country, to get the most out of living in Spain, you unquestionably need a basic level of Spanish.

In certain circumstances, such as finding a flat or giving directions to a taxi driver, it is a real help if you try to speak Spanish. Apart from these practical considerations, you will enjoy living in Spain a lot more when you can communicate. Even in the most touristy areas, there are plenty of situations in which Spanish is needed, from getting your phone connected to dealing with government officials.

How to learn Spanish

Unfortunately, despite any assertions, there are no easy tricks or shortcuts to successful learning. From language books to videocassettes to online courses, literally hundreds of companies dedicate themselves to helping people write and speak Spanish.

Read newspapers and magazines. Watch television and films. Listen to the radio. Chat with the neighbours. Constant exposure to Spanish is a necessity. The real key is simply to immerse oneself in the language and practice, practice, practice. The more you place yourself in situations where your native language cannot be used as a crutch, the quicker you will learn Spanish.

Learning in front of the television
Television is probably the quickest way to increase you level of listening comprehension. It's free and you are guaranteed to hear people speaking naturally (and fast). Don't expect to understand everything, especially things like chat-shows, as this is difficult for people with a good level of Spanish.

The more you listen and watch, the quicker you will find yourself picking up words and phrases. You will be surprised how much and how painless it can be to learn this way.

Language courses
Courses are conducted almost exclusively in Spanish, even for beginners, which should help you become accustomed to Spanish sounds and pronunciation, and therefore in order to get started, many people choose to enrol in a Spanish language course.

Between local universities offering language programs and specific language schools, there are many different options on offer.

It is generally advisable to learn at a measured pace over a longer period of time. If you need to gain a basic knowledge of Spanish in a short timeframe, these schools usually have intensive courses that will give you a "kick-start" in the language. Like any other language tool, success is purely a function of the amount of effort you put into learning. Making a concerted effort to practice your Spanish both in and outside the classroom will rapidly improve your skills.

If your time is limited or the idea of a language course doesn't appeal to you, we would still suggest having as much personal contact with Spanish people as possible. Memorizing grammar rules is wonderful but nothing beats practical experience.

Language exchanges called intercambios are the perfect way to guarantee that you practice your Spanish each week. These work by pairing up with a Spanish person that wants to learn your language. This is also a great way to make new friends.

Most universities and language schools either maintain lists of potential Spanish candidates or at least have a bulletin board with postings

Museum

The Museums of Gran Canaria covers a large part of the islands cultural and historical wealth. They includes details on everything from the islands native past to its most resent contemporary historical events.

For example, at Museo Canario in Las Palmas, visitors will find a facility containing ethnographical and archaeological collections as well as artistic creations.

At Museo de Historia de Agüimes, artefacts tell of the island's history over the last five centuries, covering events such as the establishment of the Bishop's Seat and estate (Señorío Episcopal) and the Castilian conquest of the island.

Other museums worthy of mention include Museo Elder de la Ciencia y la Tecnología, Casa Museo Pérez Galdós, and Museo Néstor all of which are located in Las Palmas. These are all worth a visit you'll have a great day out! And not to forget, most of these places are well worth a visit simply by reason of the buildings themselves, and because they are of artistic and historic importance.

Below are told about some of the more known museums. Other museums you can find under the different cities.

Casa de Colón

Colón 1, 35001 Las Palmas

Tel. 928 31 23 73

Fax. 928 33 11 56

Columbus Museum, is situated in Vequeta, the old part of Las Palmas. This Museum was opened to the public in 1950, and is placed in the former residence of the Governor, (now over 500 years old) in which Christopher Columbus lived, when he visited the Island. The building can be transported to the 15th Century.

The rooms of the museum are mainly devoted to the role played by the Canary Islands in its Discovery, and to the New World and, and you'll find Paintings from the fifteenth and sixteenth centuries and works on loan from the Prado Art gallery in Madrid.

Christopher Columbus House contains a museum and an area of scientific studies, in addition to a library that specialises in the history of America and Atlantic relations, as well as it also presents seminars, conferences and courses.

It's worth visiting for the architecture alone, which is typical of the island during that period, but there's also a permanent exhibition based around the theme of voyages of discovery and occasional temporary exhibitions.

Opening hours:

Monday - Friday 09.00 - 19.00

Saturday - Sunday 09.00 - 15.00

Closed 22 May and 24 and 31 December

Admission: Free

Casa Museo Pérez Galdos

Cano 6, 35002 Las Palmas

Tel. 928 36 69 76 / 928 37 37 45

Fax. 928 37 37 34

Casa Museo de Pérez Galdos, was the place where the famous writer wrote his things. He was born in 1894 and his house is saved as a Museum. The museumcontains the writer's complete works as well as important letters and manuscripts. Pérez Caldos lived in the house from he was born and till the year 1862.

The exhibition rooms display part of the furniture from the Galdós family houses in Madrid and Santander, as well as the Gran Canaria writer's library, archives and personal possessions. Furthermore the house representative of 18th century architecture. Every four years, the museum organises an International Congress on Galdós, also organising regular courses and seminars on the author and his times.

Opening hours:

Monday - Friday 09.00 - 21.00

Saturday - Sunday 10.00 - 15.00

Library: Monday - Friday 09.00 - 21.00

Admission: Free

Museo Canario

Dr. Verneau 2, 35001 Las Palmas

Tel. 928 33 68 00

Fax. 928 33 68 01

Museo Canario describes the Canarian past, and is founded in 1879 to you who want to know more about the Islands exciting aborigines - The Guanches. It is one the most popular and fascinating museums in Gran Canaria. There's also a big collection of skulls from the time of Cro-Magnon. A library and a newspaper archive is also at hand.

The Canarian Museum It is located in the old quarter Las Palmas and was founded in 1879. Its collection consists mostly of artefacts relating to the aboriginal people of Gran Canaria, the Canarios. It is based on the people who have inhabited the island over the centuries. Here you can see the customs and religions traditional to the island before the Spanish arrived. Every of the 11 rooms of the museum contains a different theme.

Opening hours:

Monday - Friday 10.00 - 20.00

Saturday - Sunday 10.00 - 14.00

Admission: 3,00 €

Museo Néstor

Pueblo Canario Parque Doramas

35005 Las Palmas

Tel. 928 24 51 35

Fax 928 24 35 76

The Museum displays the works of Néstor (1887-1938), one of Spain's principal symbolist painters and one of the most unusual painters of the European movement.

It is located inside the cathedral and contains the island's best treasures including important art from the 15th-18th centuries. The cathedral itself took 73 years to build and is still incomplete in parts. Tourists come here on Thursdays and Sundays to see exhibitions of Canarian dance and music.

Founded to celebrate the life and works of local artist Néstor Martin Fernandez de la Torre, this notable gallery was later extended to house further paintings from the Gallery of Contemporary Canarian Art, together with antique furniture and other local artefacts.

Opening hours:
Tuesday - Saturday 10.00 - 20.00
Sundays and Holidays 10.30-14.30
Admission: 1,80 €

Pueblo Canario
Parque Doramas, 35005 Las Palmas
Tel. 928 24 51 35
Fax 928 24 35 76

The Pueblo Canario, located in the beautiful gardens of Doramas Park in the City of Las Palmas, was created by Canarian artist Néstor de la Torre and represents the islands' typical architecture. Each Thursday and Sunday take place colourful folkloristic performances.

It was designed and built in the 1930s by the brothers Néstor and Miguel Fernandez de la Torre to interest tourists in island culture. It is a complex of several traditionally built island houses with the famous wooden carved balconies forming a typical Canary village with gates, turrets and an atrium.

The village boasts a large central square where twice a week enthusiastic folklore shows take place surrounded by shops selling local handicrafts and the Bodegón (wine bar) Canario, where you can taste several dishes of the typical Canary.

A pretty and very relaxed place in the heart of a big city, the Pueblo Canario is in spite of its obviously artificial nature well worth a visit!

Opening hours:
Tuesday - Saturday 10.00 - 20.00
Sundays and Holidays 10.30-14.30
Admission: 1,80 €

Museo Elder de la Ciencia y la Tecnologia
Parque de Santa Catalina,
35007 Las Palmas
Tel. 828 01 18 28
Fax. 828 01 10 01

Museo Elder, an impressive and well-organized science and technology museum, accommodated in a building that formerly belonged to the Elder-Dempster Shipping Line, hence the name.

In this museum, visitors to the island interested in science and technology will be entertained for hours and especially for children there are a lot of interactive exhibits to amuse them, like an industrial robot spot-welding a car just to name one of them as well as an IMAX-Cinema.

Over twenty display areas devoted to the reconstruction and reproduction of mankind's greatest scientific advances form part of this interactive science awareness centre whose motto is "Forbidden not to touch".

Opening hours:
Tuesday - Sunday 11.00 - 21.00
Admission: 3,00 €

Museo Diocesano de Arte Sacro
Espíritu Santo 20
35001 Las Palmas
Tel. 928 31 49 89
Fax. 928 31 49 89

Religious Museum situated in the south wing at the grand Cathedral de Las Palmas de Gran Canaria. The entrance is to be seen left in the picture. A visit to the museum, located in the "Patio de los Naranjos" of the Canary Islands Cathedral, is included in the entrance fee.

Items of religious art on display, including valuable sculptures and paintings from the fifteenth and sixteenth centuries as well as gold and silverware. There is an outstanding polychromatic mosaic in the Chapter House.

The museum also contains various furniture pieces that have enormous historic and artistic value.

Opening hours:
Monday - Friday
10.00 - 13.00 and 15.00 - 17.00
Admission: 1,00 €

Centro Atlantico de Arte Moderno (CAAM)
Los Balcones 9-11-13
35001 Las Palmas de Gran Canaria
Tel. 902 31 18 24
Fax. 928 32 16 29

Centro Atlántico de Arte Moderno (CAAM), is one of the City's great art centres situated in a beautiful well kept house from the 18th century. It has a permanent collection as well as hosting temporary exhibitions of modern art from around the world, and is the principal art museum of Las Palmas

Since its inauguration in 1989 the Centro Atlántico de Arte Moderno (CAAM) has become a major reference in the cultural and educational life of the islanders. Concealed behind a traditional façade, formerly belonging to a hotel, this centre is definitely worth visiting especially because of its spectacular interior design with white walls, marble stairs and acres of glass.

One of the main objectives of this Atlantic Modern Art Centre is to show the connection of Canary art with the Africa, the Americas and Europe, as the culture of the archipelago is largely determined by the influence of these three continents.

Opening hours:
Tuesday - Saturday 10.00 - 21.00
Sunday 10.00 - 14.00
Mondays and Holidays closed
Admission: Free

Casa-Museo León y Castillo

León y Castillo 43-45
35200 Telde
Tel. 928 69 13 77
Fax. 928 69 66 53

An institution established in 1954 by the council of Gran Canaria, situated in the house in which two distinguished Gran Canaria personalities were born, namely Fernando León y Castillo, the first marquis of Muni, and his brother, Juan, the engineer who designed the port named Puerto de la Luz in Las Palmas, and who was a faithful exponent of Mudejar architecture in the Canaries. Both men were faithful exponents of the political class of the Bourbon Restoration.

The museum houses a research centre, with a library that is specialised in contemporary history. This centre organises courses, seminars and conferences, while also awarding scholarships and a research prize.

Museo Palacio Spínola

The house of the Spínola family is one of the most important surviving buildings in the town owing both to its features and to its size. It was built by Don José Feo Peraza between 1730 and 1780, though his son Don José Feo de Armas was the most important person to live in this mansion. The surname Spínola became associated with the mansion for the first time in its history in 1895, after being linked to the Feo family for over 150 years.

The house-museum León y Castillo is one of the best examples of large ancestral houses in Canarias. Inside the house, there are numerous personal objects, the library and paintings by Gusach, Raimundo Madrazo and José Arencibia Gil. Other places of interest are the tower of Gando, of the 18th century, at present aeronautical museum, the ancestral houses of the quarter of San Juan, with their carving works of Arucas and wooden balconies coloured in green, the house of Ponce de León and the so called basilica menor.

Telde possesses the oldest historical centre in the whole canary archipelago. The natural environment of Telde is of great beauty. Most interesting is the Special Natural Reservation of Los Marteles, with places of great importance like el barranco de los Cernícalos or el barranco de las Goteras, in the protected landscape of Tafira.

Opening hours:
Monday - Friday 08.00 - 20.00
Saturday - Sunday 10.00 - 13.00
Admission: Free

Casa Museo Tomás Morales
Plaza Tomás Morales
35420 Moya
Tel. 928 62 02 17 / 928 61 24 01
Fax. 928 61 12 17

The birthplace of the modernist poet Tomás Morales(1884-1921). Numerous personal possessions and pieces of furniture belonging to the poet are on display together with editions of all of his works and those of other Canary Islands poets. And a yearly poetry competition, which is well supported.

The museum has a library that specialises in poetry, while also organising various cultural activities, such as conferences, concerts and recitals... It also awards a prize for poetry, in addition to scholarships and a research prize

The museum's holdings consist of objects or memorabilia closely linked to the author, and are based on the writer's legacy.

Opening hours:
Monday - Friday 09.00 - 20.00
Saturday 10.00 - 20.00
Sundays and Holidays 10.00 - 14.00
Admission: Free

Casa-Museo de Antonio Padrón
Drago 2
35460 Gáldar
Tel. 928 55 18 58
Fax. 928 55 18 58

The Antonio Padrón house-museum in Gáldar is located in the painters former studio and belongs to a larger architectural complex that included the family dwelling, which is now separate from the museum premises.

Here, you can contemplate more than a hundred works by a Canarian artist, being one of the most representative artists of the indigenous movement.

Opening hours:
Monday - Friday 09.00 - 14.00

Archaeological Museum

Plaza de San Antón 1

35260 Agüimes

Tel. 928 78 54 53

For four centuries, Agüimes was a domain of the Episcopal Chamber; the Episcopal Palace witnessed that period. The first writing mention to this building as Palacio de Obispos (Bishop's Palace) dates from 1706. Said building has been restored and now houses the long-waited Museum of Agüimes History.

The Agüimes History Museum enables visitors to learn about the last five centuries of the area's history, from the establishment of the Señorío Episcopal (Bishop's Seat and estate), following the Castilian Conquest of the island, up until the middle of the 20th century.

Interspersed between the different exhibition rooms and the services provided by the museum, are architectural works, some of which are new, while others have been recently restored.

This doubtless helps to recover the former splendour of such a unique building. In addition, the generosity of the town's residents in ceding many of the items on display has not only prevented them from being lost but also has allowed them to be enjoyed by all.

Nowadays the museum has eight rooms for exhibiting the historical legacy: Episcopal Domain; Territory, and Population; Social Classes; Migrations, and Social Problems; Ideas; Home Economics; Agricultural-Ranching Economy, and Industry; Craftsmanship and Commerce.

Opening hours:
Tuesday - Sunday
08.30 - 13.30 & 16.00 - 18.00
Monday closed
Admission: 2,50 €

Museo de Guayadeque
(Centro de interpretación arqueológica)
Barranco de Guayadeque
35260 Agüimes
Tel. 928 17 20 26

The Guayadeque ravine is situated between the towns of Agüimes and Ingenio, in the east of Gran Canaria island. The ravine can be reached by road from both towns passing through the troglodyte hamlet of Cueva Bermeja and ending at the small village of Montaña de las Tierras situated within the ravine.

The outstanding environmental and heritage value of this exceptional area has led to it being declared a Natural Monument in accordance with the Law for Natural Areas of the Canaries and as an Area of Cultural Interest with the classification of Archaeological Site.

The preservation of this natural and cultural wealth has been possible due to the isolation this area has been subjected to up until relatively recently and this has also permitted the endurance of centuries old traditions and practices in the area which have long disappeared from other parts of the island.

In its course of some 20 km, from the foothills of the Marteles crater to the area surrounding the El Burrero beach, the water has carved out a channel and created towering walls in which a considerable number of typical Canarian plants have their home. The diverse flora and fauna benefit from the variety of altitudes and temperatures which occur along the water course of the ravine, from its headwaters in the peak district to the point at which it reaches the coast, through the areas in between.

The water, which has helped to shape this relief, has been and continues to be one of the defining elements of the landscape and of the ways of life in the ravine. The different sources have not only encouraged the growth of vegetation but have also provided sufficient water to cultivate adjacent land plots and supply the surrounding villages.

Human activity in this area dates from the Pre-Hispanic Age, an age from which we have many reports. The archaeological importance of Guayadeque began to be recognised in the last decades of the 19th century, when the Museo Canario began the first explorations.

The mummies and the large burial caves are the most well-known archaeological elements of the ravine but they are by no means the only ones. Modern archaeology, in addition to the further study of anthropological and burial aspects, has highlighted the presence of other equally significant elements such as the large troglodyte hamlets, grain stores and the cave paintings and engravings.

When post-Conquest historical documentation refers to Guayadeque it does so almost exclusively in relation to the exploitation of the waters whether for supply and irrigation or to drive the mills which have lain along its route up until the present day.

Guaydeque's environmental resources of national importance are on show in the Information Centre, situated in a building that has been carved out of the hillside following the troglodyte tradition of the ravine. The centre allows you to journey from the depths of the past when erosion and volcanic activity first shaped this route to its current state, through the indigenous occupation and subsequent settlement.

Opening hours:
Tuesday - Saturday 09.00 -17.00
Sunday 10.00 - 18.00
Monday closed
Admission: 2,50 €

Parque Arqueológico de Cueva Pintada
Audiencia 2
35460 Gáldar
Tel. 928 89 57 46
Fax. 928 55 24 02

After having been closed for 24 years, while work was performed and a gentle modernization was made, Cueva Pintada was reopened on the 27. of July 2006. The famous cave now appears a modern Museum

Complex, showing a unique, historic part of Gran Canaria. Many people will visit, tourists as well as locals, and it is a must-do visit.

Cueva Pintada is a small cave with geometric paintings from the Guanches, which is unique on the island. It is located in the small town Gáldar, which was the seat of Gran Canarias ancient rulers at the time of conquest in 1478. The Spanish city was built over the aboriginal settlement and the cave lost.

The cave has several rooms which were used as cave houses by the Guanche. Several walls were built from basalt or tufa without mortar. Bed and seat were also carved out of the soft rock.

In the caves mummies, tools and pottery were found. But the most famous finds were the drawings, that gave the cave its name. The paintings are red, black, and white squares, spirals, and triangles. The meaning of the paintings is not clear, some imagine symbols of female fertility the expression of religious beliefs. But maybe they are just simply for decoration.

This drawings/paintings are bleaching by the light, so the cave was closed several years ago. Another problem is irrigation water, oozing though the volcanic ash rock of the cave, is raising the humidity and destroys the paint.

The whole site, the cave and the ruins of the surrounding village, were restored during the last years. The paintings were covered by a special glass to protect them. A new museum was created, which shows the findings and - as a part of the visit - the view into the cave.

However, it is not possible to enter the cave, just a visit through the protecting glass is possible. There are computers in the museum which allow a virtual cave visit, and there is a new website which also allows a virtual visit. The virtual visit is a computer animated mpeg file though, and is obviously generated by the architect of the new museum building. Hopefully they will find the means to change this soon, now the museum is reopened.

Opening hours:
Tuesday - Saturday 09.00 -17.00
Sunday 10.00 - 18.00
Monday closed
Admission: 2,50 €

Mundo Aborigen
Parque Natural de Ayagaures
Carretera Playa del Inglés - Fataga, Km 6
Tel. 928 17 22 95

Mundo Aborigen is an outdoor Museum on at least 110.000 m². In a protected National Park, a setting of incomparable beauty, and through a carefully planned itinerary we will se before our very eyes the different aspects of their life: the social hierarchy, the world of magic and religion, burial rites, the most deeply rooted social customs, different types of dwellings, ornamentation, manual skills, food, agriculture and live animals.

All of which is presented with more than one hundred life-size figures showing the aborigines in a setting of a large variety of endemic flora which make the visit even more pleasant. In order to pay special attention to the most important aspects, we have created a small archaeological museum which, together with the different shows and demonstrations of the island's sports, complete this fascinating visit.

Mundo Aborigen has been declared, "A place of Cultural, Social and Historical Interest" by the Canarian Government.

Unfortunately there are no shows or such, as was the case in the beginning, and the adjoining kiosk is closed, so you'll have to bring your own food and drink.

Opening hours:
Monday - Sunday 09.00 - 18.00
Admission: 10 € - Children free

Castillo de la Luz

Calle Juan Rejón
35007 Las Palmas
Tel. 928 46 47 57

This fortress defended the natural harbour of Las Palmas for several centuries. The name means Castle of Light. It is located on the southern coast of La Isleta, and was built in 1541 on the foundations of an old fort from the time of the conquest by the Castilians.

The solid fortress was equipped with a platform for eleven cannons. But it suffered severe damages during the invasion of Dutch pirates in 1599 and burnt out completely. The Castillo de la Luz defended the natural harbour of Las Palmas de Gran Canaria for several centuries.

During the following centuries the two-storey building was rebuilt, extended and improved. In 1941 the Castillo de la Luz was declared a national historic monument. This well-preserved fortress was restored in 1990 and serves today as a cultural and exhibition centre, for national and international events.

Cenobio de Valerón

Cuesta de Silva
35450 Santa María de Guía
Tel. 928 21 94 21

Cenobio de Valerón is a large basaltic arch, covering volcanic tuff. Into this rather soft material, the Guanche excavated about 300 caves, cavities and cubicles.

These cave are fascinating. To this day, nobody really knows why they are here... The Monastery of Caves are located on the north coast of Gran Canaria. They date back to the Stone Age and are widely recognised as the most important and impressive pieces of architecture on the island.

In total there are 298 caves here. It's considered a very holy place. But the question remains... who were the original inhabitants and why were they there?

Many people believe that it was a monastery or "cenebio" where young girls went in preparation of marriage, in order to practice spiritual exercises and perform various rituals. Others say the caves were just used as granaries. Whatever they were used for, they certainly are very impressive to look at!

This place is an agadir (a collective-fortificated granary) similar to the agadirs in North Africa. The ancient people stored their agricultural surplus here. The Faican, a religious, political and economic chief distributed it between the community.

The cavities were used as silos, closed with a wooden plank and marked with a seal called pintadera that indicated the owner.

The visitors reach this place in a few minutes from the well developed coastal highway. A small road winds along a steep valley and runs right below the cenobio. The small parking is only suitable for half a dozen cars, but it seems the typical Gran Canaria tourist is not interested to visit this place, and the this small parking is absolutely sufficient.

From the car the road is crossed to fence with a sort of ticket office at the fence. The guard tells you something about protection of the site and helps with some archaeological background info. But there is no fee and you are free to visit the whole site, as long as you stay on the paved paths.

This site, along with the Gáldar Painted Cave, is one of the most important relics of the heritage of Native Islanders prior to Spanish conquest.

To get to the caves, take the C-810 road to Las Palmas heading east of Guia until you get to Cuesta de Silva. Then just take the road up to the car park. You can walk up to the caves from here.

Opening hours:
Tuesday - Sunday

Sam Kennedy

10.00 - 13.00 & 15.00 - 17.00

Admission: Free

Travel and Tourism
Things to Do

Gran Canaria has more than 80 beaches, from well-equipped resorts to untamed and wonderfully hidden strips of precious sand. But the island has much more to offer beyond beaches. There is a never-ending list of what to see and do in Las Palmas de Gran Canaria. Below is a guide to typical places and secluded things to enjoy doing during your visit to the island.

Roque Nublo: Roque Nublo is a volcanic rock standing 80 meters tall. It is a famous landmark of the island, protected by UNESCO as a natural monument. Located in the municipality Tejeda, a short ride from the city center, it came into existence after a volcanic eruption approximately 4.5 million years ago. Roque Nublo is the most popular destination in Gran Canaria for hiking lovers, and would be an ideal experience for all who desire to see the wonderful views of Tejeda mountain. The usual starting point for a hike in Nublo is the area of

Degollada de la Goleta, which is reached by vehicle, and is where hikers descend following a clearly signposted trail.

Tejeda, Las Palmas, Gran Canaria, +34 928 666 001

Maspalomas: Maspalomas is the second longest beach in Gran Canaria, and is primarily famous for its vast dunes that often grace the covers of travel guides of Canary Islands. However, dunes are a fragile ecosystem, and need to be visited with care. There are three walking routes available for curious visitors, with signposts and information available at the information point at the Playa del Inglés. The highlight of your visit will be an opportunity to ride a camel in the desert and stop by lagoon with fresh crystal clear water.

San Bartolomé de Tirajana, Maspalomes, Gran Canaria

Jardín Botánico Viera y Clavijo: Jardín Botánico Viera y Clavijo, located in the northeast of Gran Canaria, in Tafira Alta, proves that Gran Canaria is not as deserted and dry as it seems. The botanic garden showcases the island's endemic plants, alongside some imported flora. The bust of José de Viera y Clavijo, the Spanish botanist who had an idea of opening a botanic garden on the Canary Islands, proudly welcomes all visitors. The garden has collected about 500 plant species, endemic to the Canary Islands and other Macaronesian islands, with cacti and succulent varieties are available to look at on display. The garden contributes heavily to the program of species preservation through its research work. Its facilities include a library and laboratories, and it also publishes the journal Botánica Macaronésica.

Opening hours: 9am-6pm daily

Ctra. del Centro, Km 7, Las Palmas de Gran Canaria, Las Palmas, +34 928 21 95 80

Pueblo Canario: The city of Las Palmas de Gran Canaria is a home to the Pueblo Canario, an interpretation of a traditional Canarian village. Pueblo Canario is located on the south side of the Parque Doramas and it is a lovely venue to visit with family, and learn more about Spanish culture from free live performances of Canarian folk music, which are held every Thursday and Sunday. Some songs performed are instrumental, while others include live singing. All performers wear special traditional costumes which are pleasant to look at. Pueblo Canario also houses the Museo Néstor, one of the city's principal art galleries.

Opening hours: 8am-12am daily

Calle Francisco González Díaz, Las Palmas de Gran Canaria, +34 928 24 29 85

Stroll around Puerto Mogan: Puerto Mogan is a coastal village, located on the southern side of the island, the opposite side to Las Palmas de Gran Canaria. It is a charming small village which never gets too loud, and its small beach is a peaceful refuge where you can recharge your energy. Puerto Mogan oozes a chic ambiance, thanks to its uniform white architecture, beautiful flower gardens and little bridges over the canals. All of this makes a visit to Puerto Mogán a romantic holiday experience.

Callejon Explanada del Castillete, Mogán, Las Palmas de Gran Canaria

Vegueta: Vegueta is an ancient 15th century town, full of memories and secret stories of its maritime past, that is comprised of traditional Spanish architecture, cobbled streets and old houses. Vegueta is not a uniform part of the city, as it was built according to a range of styles, from late-Gothic to renaissance. Walk through the Plaza de Santa Ana to see the principal landmark of Vegueta, the Cathedral of Santa Ana. The Museum of Sacred Art is also not to be missed. There are also important art galleries, including the Centro de Cultura Contemporánea San Martín and Casa de Colon, dedicated to the life of Christopher Columbus. After the walk, head to one of the traditional restaurants and sample a typical tapas of the Canarian islands, such as papas arrugadas, local cheeses and pata de cerdo.

Vegueta, Las Palmas de Gran Canaria

Sioux City: Sioux City is a Western-style theme park located in San Bartolome de Tirajana, near San Agustin. Sioux City is situated in a unique natural environment, in a cactus-filled canyon. All objects and art performances are an exact replica of the American Wild-West. The theme park offers a number of thrilling attractions for visitors, where they can experience the Wild West. Sioux City offers a variety of fun, exciting shows covering Western themes, with Indians and cowboys, duels and chases that will not leave children and adults alike unamused.

Opening hours: Tue-Sun 10am-5pm

Barranco del Aguila, San Bartolomé de Tirajana, Gran Canarias, +34 928 762 982

See a film at Moonlight Cinema: Located on the top floor of the shopping mall in Maspalomas, Moonlight Cinema is Europe's only permanent outdoor cinema. It invites you to relax and enjoy the bright films on the big screen under the magic of the stars and warm surroundings of Gran Canaria. The interior features luxurious sofas, blankets and fantastic service available at the push of the button on your seat. There is a selection of fresh delicious stonebaked pizza, popcorn and nachos to indulge on. A blanket is provided on each seat to make sure that no one will feel uncomfortable against the evening chill.

Opening hours: Mon-Thu 9am-3pm and 7pm-1am, Fri-Sat 7pm-1am Avenida Cristobal Colon, San Bartolome de Tirajana, Maspalomas, Gran Canaria, +34 677 27 03 10

Get extreme with water sports: There are plenty water sports activities that can be done during your stay in Gran Canaria, as the Canary Islands are an ideal place to try that particular water sport you resisted for a long time. You are free to choose from activities such as sailing, yachting, windsurfing, water-skiing, scuba diving and much more. Windsurfing in Gran Canaria is the most popular activity, because the warm air and water temperature are a perfect combination, with the wind blowing from the eastern side of the island

Attractions Gran Canaria

With explosive surf and sizzling volcanic sand beaches, Gran Canaria is one hot destination for weekend breaks. Here's what to do on this beautiful little island

Scuba in Gran Canaria

Gran Canaria boasts incredible biodiversity, both above and below sea level, so take the plunge with a scuba dive to see an impressive variety of marine life. Get up close and personal with a manta ray or sea turtle, or lose yourself just gazing at the remarkable colours of fish and crustaceans found in abundance at sites like the El Cabrón Marine Reserve. If you're feeling adventurous, tackle a submerged wreck at Puerto Mogan or the dramatic La Catedral cave dive at Las Palmas. You'll be in good hands with experienced dive centres such as Davy Jones Diving or the Gran Canaria Dive Academy. What's more, the island's turquoise-hued waters couldn't be more inviting, with a year-round temperature of 23 degrees C.

Ride sand dunes on camelback

Make like Lawrence of Arabia in Maspalomas, a glorious 8km-long white beach featuring colossal dunes that span half its length and extend a further 3.5km inland. Sure you can walk, horse ride or even quad bike these 404 hectares of rolling sand hills, but for something out of the ordinary, take a camel ride. The camels' long legs mean there's a different rhythm it's a slower pace than on horseback and strangely calming. Playing safari in this mini Sahara is hot work, so cool down with a sorbet in the shadow of the magnificent 56-feet-tall Maspalomas lighthouse. The promenade is the place to people watch at sunset, and if you're lucky you'll catch the beach's resident sand artist hard at work crafting his next sculpture.

Opening Hours: Daily tours - organise directly with Camel Safari Tickets: €35 per adult, €19 per child Address: GC-60, Km. 14, 35108 Fataga, Las Palmas

Hike Caldera de Bandama

This Jurassic bowl-shaped crater evokes prehistoric times. At 1000 metres in diameter and 200 metres deep, this awesome crater was formed by an extremely powerful volcanic eruption an estimated 1,970 years ago. It looks formidable, but you can hike down into the crater comfortably in 30 minutes; allow double the time to get back up though. It goes without saying that you should wear sturdy boots and carry plenty of water. Walking the cinder path you'll see lizards, cacti, eucalyptus and orange trees, while the view from the platform atop the crater extends over the entire north-east and central mountainous belt of the island. You can get food and drink at the nearby golf club, but as this is vineyard territory, you may want to enjoy the harvest of the Vino Del Monte with a well-earned glass of Rioja.

Opening Hours: 24 hours Tickets: Free Address: Santa Brigida, 35300 Las Palmas de Gran Canaria, Gran Canaria, Spain

Moonwalk at Roque Nublo

Bang in the centre of the island, this little and large rock pairing is well worth a visit. The relatively short hike up to this unmistakable landmark is hot work, so get hydrated with a fresh juice from the van in the car park. Standing 80 metres tall and 1,813 meters above sea level, the Roque Nublo isn't actually the highest point on the island (that accolade goes to Pico de la Nieves), although with its exposed position rising out of the Caldera de Tejeda, it is certainly the most prominent. You can enjoy panoramic 360-degree views of the island from on top of the peak, but the quasi-lunar landscape itself is the real draw: it's quite uncanny.

Opening Hours: 24 hours Tickets: Free Address: GC150, 35368, Gran Canaria

Go stargazing

Is there life on Mars? Thanks to the island's position on the equator, low-level cloud phenomena that filter out light pollution and a law that regulates air traffic, Gran Canaria is one of the best places in Europe from which to see the stars. The unusually clear and bright skies allow for cracking views of constellations found in both northern and southern hemispheres. Vantage points such as Temisas Astronomic Observatory and Roque Saucillo Astronomy Centre offer informative night walks along with top-flight views of the stars. If you're holidaying with your partner, a night spent staring at the heavens makes for a perfect romantic evening.

Surf like a Big Kahuna

The coastline of Pozo Izquierdo plays host to some seriously impressive surf. Sit on the sand and watch as the boards and sails cut and glide through the water, or if you want to have a go yourself, check in with the friendly staff of one many local surfing schools, who will make getting started a breeze. With a little practice you'll be upright and cruising in no time. Be warned though, once you've successfully surfed your first swell, you'll find the experience is addictive so be sure to pack a few pairs of board shorts. As they say in surf speak, totally excellent, dude.

Address: Av. las Bajas, 73, 35119 Pozo Izquierdo, Las Palmas

Study ancient cave paintings

The Cueva Pintida Museum is built around an archeological excavation site that dates back to pre-Hispanic times. There's an elevated walkway that allows you to look down into the extraordinary site, and effectively back in time, as far as the Paleolithic era. The cave paintings are also worth a look, as they provide a fascinating insight into the types of symbolism and iconography used by the indigenous aboriginal people long before European colonization. All visits to the museum are guided, so to avoid disappointment book an appointment in advance.

Opening Hours: 10am-6pm daily, 11am-6pm Sundays, closed on Mondays Tickets: €6 per adult, €4 per child Address: Calle Audiencia, 2, 35460 Gáldar, Las Palmas

Follow in Christopher Columbus's footsteps at Casa-Museo de Colón

Did Christopher Columbus stay here in 1492? Even if he didn't, many of the first governors of the island did, and this impressive palace, a prime example of Canarian architecture, is a must-see. Intricate Gothic metalwork and ornate fountains set the scene outside, and inside the wow factor continues: explore the 13 exhibition rooms, library and study centre. Chart the epic voyages of the famous navigator, trace journeys across large nautical maps and step into a replica of the cabin of *La Nina*, one of the ships Columbus used in his voyage across to the West Indies.

Opening Hours: 10am-6pm daily, 10am-3pm Sundays Tickets: €4 per adult, €2 per child Address: Calle Colón, 1, 35001 Las Palmas de Gran Canaria, Las Palmas

Sup Arucas rum

Five centuries of sugar cane cultivation has given the Canaries a sweet tooth. It wasn't long before this tendency led to the creation of rum, first sweetened with sugar cane honey and then bee's honey. Nowadays, in Gran Canaria, Arucas rum is ubiquitous and is exported worldwide. A visit to the distillery, 15 minutes journey from the capital Las Palmas, is a very merry way to spend an afternoon. Every year, more than 3.5 million litres of rum are produced here; see the rum production process before sampling one of the many flavours, from banana and coffee to honey and toffee. And don't miss the celebrity autographs on the casks.

Opening Hours: 9am-1pm, closed on the weekends Tickets: €6 per person Address: Lugar Era de San Pedro, 2, 35400 Arucas, Las Palmas

Experience the Gran Canaria Carnival

As you may have guessed from all that rum, the Gran Canarians love to party, and aren't shy of a festival or two. By far the biggest event of the calendar year is the Carnival, an explosively colourful street parade held every February, in the spirit of the Rio Carnival or Sydney's Mardi Gras. There is a whole week of events, including the Queen Gala and Drag Queen Gala, and of course the annual closing ritual, which involves the elaborate burying of a sardine. Grieving 'widows' dressed in black hoist a giant effigy of a sardine in a procession down to the shore, then load it onto a boat and burn it at sea. As you do.

Opening Hours: Usually the last week of February Address: Las Palmas, Gran Canaria

Have a grand day out in Palmitos Park

Palmitos is the biggest zoological park in the Canary Islands, with hundreds of ocean dwellers like dolphins, turtles, seals, reptiles, lories, toucans and pelicans calling it home. There's a schedule of feeding times, shows and demonstrations every day, and for just €60, you can spend time with one of the dolphins in a hands on lesson about the species in the water. Aqualand is also 10 minutes away, if you'd prefer slides to seals.

Opening Hours: 10am-6pm daily Tickets: £26 per adult online, £19 per child Address: Barranco de los Palmitos, s/n, 35109 Maspalomas, Las Palmas, Spain

Sip a cocktail on Playa de Las Canteras

If you came away for a beach holiday, plant yourself onto Playa de Las Canteras. This is where the crowds come to sunbathe, people watch and bodyboard to their hearts content. You'll usually find sand sculptures hiding between the deckchairs, and there's no better way to spend an evening that nursing a mojito on the promenade, watching the surfers come in.

Address: Paseo de las Canteras, Las Palmas de Gran Canaria, Las Palmas de Gran Canaria, Gran Canaria

Get artsy at Museo Néstor

Néstor's museum and art gallery makes a cool change to the hot weather and beautiful beaches in Gran Canaria. Marvel at Nestor's earliest work, 1900's Marina, which he finished when he was just 13 years old. The Canarian artist used to live in the San Francisco district of Teide, however, he passed away before he was able to catalogue his work properly. His brother went onto build Museo Néstor - a gem of a museum in Las Palmas.

Opening Hours: 10am-7pm daily, Sundays 10.30am-2.30pm Tickets: 0.50 cents per person Address: Calle Francisco González Díaz, s/n, 35005 Las Palmas de Gran Canaria, Las Palmas

Relax in the Viera y Clavijo Botanical Garden

This garden was named after the scholar Jose Viera y Clavijo after he attempted to found the Canary's first botanical garden in the eighteenth century, but failed. It was Erik Ragnar Svensson who found this spot, which is able to hold all of the Canary Islands different plant species. There are 600 unique plants in this garden - try to spot them all.

Opening Hours: 9am-6pm Tickets: Free Address: Ctra. del Centro, Km 7, 35017 Las Palmas de Gran Canaria, Las Palmas, Spain

Chill out at Arguineguín

Stand-up paddle, surf or scuba in Arguineguín - this is the seaside town of the wave riders in Gran Canaria. Their local market takes place on a Tuesday, where you can buy local crafts, trinkets and snacks from the island. Learn how to do stand-up paddle boarding with Patalasup, and spend the rest of the afternoon in one of the bars or one of Canaria's hookah lounges.

Address: Arguineguín, Las Palmas, Gran Canaria

Tour Recommendations

Palmitos Park

Barranco Los Palmitos s/n.

Aptdo. 107 Maspalomas.

San Bartolomé de Tirajana

Tel. 928 14 02 76

Fax. 928 14 11 58

Mail. pp@aspro-ocio.es

Gran Canaria's most popular family attraction, the Palmitos Park, is a subtropical oasis in a verdant valley of palm trees, featuring more than 200 species of birds, including the tiny hummingbirds, toucans, peacocks, hornbills, cranes, flamingos and macaws among other attractions such as an aquarium, a butterfly house, a cactus garden, an orchid house...

Palmitos Park boasts a lot of 'must see' attractions and you should count with at least a couple of hours or even half a day to wander around the park and take in all the sights and sounds, or watch the breathtaking bird of prey shows, where eagles, owls and peregrine falcons will swoop down over the audience in free flight.

Another spectacular attraction not to be missed are the parrot shows, where you see these intelligent birds perform an amazing variety of tricks, from riding bicycles to doing jigsaws, painting pictures and counting to ten.

Other attractions are the Orchid House, the Cactus Garden, the Butterfly House is the biggest in all Europe, with hundreds of exotic butterflies flying freely a truly unforgettable experience.

The Aquarium features a wide variety of tropical fishes. Salt and freshwater fishes with most amazing colours and shapes live in a recreated riverbed. Gibbon Island, home to some white-handed gibbons, whose natural habitats are the Malayan Peninsula and Burma and who have been successfully bred here, the first time in captivity. All of this is set within more than 1,000 palm trees and 15,000 plants, representing an abundance of endemic and imported species.

Cocodrilo Park

Carretera Gral Los Corralillos

Villa de Aguimes Gran Canaria

Tel. +34 928 78 47 25

Fax. +34 928 78 47 18

Mail. cocodrilpark@hotmail.com

It all started when the Balser family was asked to take care of a few crocodiles... They did, and now they have the largest collection in Europe. The organisation SEPRONA (Environmental Protection Police) has placed many animals in the Balser family's capable hands. These animals chimpanzees, various monkeys, birds, among many others arrived usually in very bad health conditions.

This was the start of the Parque de los Cocodrilos, Gran Canaria's only zoological park. It was first opened to the public in 1988. In the following years the family continuously added animals to the park by buying them from private people and circuses, and now there are about 300 crocodiles, and species of tropical fishes, the 'Parrot Show on the Treasure Island', a cacti garden are just some of the attractions you will see in this unusual animal park.

The upkeep of this ever-growing park and the salaries for its professional and caring staff are supported with the income from the entrance fees.

Opening hours: Sunday to Friday from 10.00 to 18.00

Entré adults 10 € - children 7 €

Holiday World

Avda. Touroperador TUI

35100 Maspalomas

Tel. 928 73 04 98

Fax. 928 76 67 25

The Holiday World leisure and amusement park has been completely rebuilt and since it was reopened, it has already become very popular with both visitors and locals, especially at weekends.

The new Holiday World boasts a traditional fun fair featuring numerous exciting attractions such as a classic 27 meters high Ferris wheel, a roller coaster, a laserdrome, shooting stalls, seal and parrot shows and many more things to entertain the kids. It also comprises a leisure centre including a bowling alley, amusement arcades, a 'wellness centre' with a health spa and a high-tech gym, various cafés and restaurants as well as two night clubs (one of which is a salsa club), which already attract huge crowds at the weekends.

More for daytime use, you'll find a five-minute walk away a large park featuring a boating lake, children playgrounds, pony riding, and a karting track… only to mention some of the attractions offered there.

Opening hours: Major attractions from 18.00 to 24.00 hrs; 'wellness centre' also during daytime; park during daytime; night clubs open up to early morning hours.
Location: Campo International in Maspalomas Gran Canaria's

Opening hours:
Sunday - Thursday 18.00 - 24.00
Friday and Saturday 18.00 - 01.00

Opening Hours of the Bowling Alley:
Sunday - Thursday 10.00 - 02.00
Friday 10.00 - 03.00
Saturday 10.00 - 04.00

Mundo Aborigen

Parque Natural de Ayagaures

Carretera Playa del Inglés - Fataga, Km 6

Tel. 928 17 22 95

Mundo Aborigen is a outdoor Museum on at least 110.000 m². In a protected National Park, a setting of incomparable beauty, and through a carefully planned itinerary we will se before our very eyes the different aspects of their life: the social hierarchy, the world of magic and religion, burial rites, the most deeply rooted social customs, different types of dwellings, ornamentation, manual skills, food, agriculture and live animals.

All of which is presented with more than one hundred life-size figures showing the aborigines in a setting of a large variety of endemic flora which make the visit even more pleasant. In order to pay special attention to the most important aspects, we have created a small archaeological museum which, together with the different shows and demonstrations of the island's sports, complete this fascinating visit.

Aborigen World has been declared, "A place of Cultural, Social and Historical Interest" by the Canarian Goverment.

Unfortunately there are no shows or such, as was the case in the beginning, and the adjoining kiosk is closed, so you'll have to bring your own food and drink.

Opening Hours: Monday through Sunday 09.00 - 18.00

Entré adults 10 € - Children free

Sioux City

Barranco del Águila, s/n.

35107 San Agustín, Maspalomas, Gran Canaria.

Tel. +34 928 762 982

Ride back in time and get the feel of the 'roaring Wild West'! Meet mythical warriors like White Herb and cowboys such as Doc Holiday or get caught in a bank hold up or a sudden shoot-out between cold-blooded cowpokes and the lawmen of Sioux City... This is a recreation of the American Wild West with gunfights, rustic barbecues, saloon gals, sheriffs and can-can girls... and to make the feel complete the air around you is filled with country & western music.

There are plenty of attractions to watch such as 'duel until death', 'bank robbery', 'saloon fight', 'town square hanging', 'Indian rain dance' and Mexican acrobats performing stunts involving lassos, whips and knives... just to name some.

Covering a surface of 320.000 m², this park is a replica of a Wild West town with its typical houses, a church, a ranch, a bank and a saloon. And of course, where you see cowboys there also must be Indians... So don't miss the Indian reservation! For the kiddies (as if that wasn't already enough) there is a small zoo with some cute animals. A fascinating attraction for both young and old... don't miss it!

This place was originally built for an American western in the 1970's and has later been developed as a Wild West theme park. Every Friday there is a special barbecue evening, and if you want to visit the park it's good to go on a Friday to catch the barbecue as well.

Opening hours: from 10.00 to 17.00 except on Mondays

Admission: Adults 21,90 € - Children 15,90 €

Friday Night open at 20.00 for a Barbecue night and 90 min.

Fantastic "wild west show"

Admission: Adults 52 € - Children 22 €

Residents -30%

Cactualdea Parque

Carreera del Hoyo, Tocodomán

35478 La Aldea de San Nicolás

Tel. 928 89 12 28

Fax. 928 89 06 88

E-Mail: **catuald@intercom.es**

Cactualdea - Is a cactus park, very popular with tourists. Here you can see 1200 different species of cacti imported from countries like Mexico, Madagascar, Guatemala and Bolivia, set between palms, dragon trees and aloes.

There is also a model Guanche Cave there and a nice restaurant where you can enjoy a relax over a typical meal from the Canary Islands or choose from the international dishes before visiting the animals (camels, ostriches, goats, peacocks).

Other points of interest are a large amphitheatre that is used for Luchas Canarias, Canary wrestling matches (two people wearing shorts wrestle in a way that is similar to the wrestling that takes place in the Far East), and a wine cellar with 250 types of wine to be tasted.

Open daily 10.00 - 18.00
Entré adults 6 € - 13-18 year 3 € and children under 13 years go in for free.

Camel Safari

Although it might sound strange (going on a camel ride in Gran Canaria, as opposed to getting drunk beside the pool!) this is a very popular activity and is getting more so every year.

The best place for camelback excursions is the famous Sahara-like sand dunes of Maspalomas. You can watch the setting sun and pretend you're Lawrence of Arabia, on top of your exotic dromedary!

Another good place where rides are available is beside a pretty little village called Fataga. The guides will tell you all you need to know about how you ride a camel. Then you'll get to ride one of these fascinating animals through the beautiful valley of Fataga.

Gokart

Spend an unforgettable day in Gran Canaria's two Go-carts track. Gran Karting Club is the biggest Go-carts Track in Spain, and there are Go-carts to adults as well as children. The karts to the children have got speed-reducers so they only can drive 35 - 40 km/h. There is also small motorcycles not more than about 40 cm. above earth level.

Jardín Botánico

Barranco de Guiniguada

Tafira Alta

"The Canary Garden", Jardin Botanical" is situated in Tafira Alta about 10 minutes driving from Las Palmas. It is the biggest botanical garden in Spain. The garden covers about 27 hectares and is founded in 1952 by the Swede Eric Sventenius.

When you enter the garden one of the first places to se is Plaza Viera y Clavijo, from where you can see all of the garden, which by the way contain more than 2000 kinds of cactus, waterfalls, lakes and much more.

Many of the plants are unique for the Canary Island, and many botanists go to the Islands from the same reason. In order to secure natural environments the garden is situated in a undulated ground.
Opening Hours daily 10.00 - 18.00 - Closed on all holidays

Sport & Leisure

Air Sport

If you are more of the adventurous type and love the feeling of freedom and weightlessness, there are several locations on Gran Canaria that provide perfect conditions for all types of wind and air sports.

The island's mountainous terrain and almost constant Trade Winds allow the practice of such new sports include:
Skydiving, Parachuting, Hang-gliding, Paragliding and Flying.

There are plenty of companies on the island, which offer these services, very often including courses both for beginners and advanced.

For flying, parachuting, hang-gliding or paragliding contact some of the advertisers below.

Federación Canaria de Deportes Aéreos	http://www.fecda.org
Jump for Life	http://www.jump-for-life.com
Skydive Gran Canaria	http://www.skydivegrancanaria.es
Paraclub de Gran Canaria	http://www.paraclubdegrancanaria.com
Real Aeroclub de Gran Canaria	http://www.aeroclubgrancanaria.com
Club de Parapente La Alpispa	

Cycling

Gran Canaria is a paradise for lovers of bicycle touring and nature. If you like downhill cycling or long-distance routes, the bicycle and the enormous variety of routes which the Island offers are a perfect combination to get to know indescribable spots.

Gran Canaria is also a paradise for Mountain bikers. Mountain biking is a form of cycling which uses very sturdy bicycles with (usually) straight handlebars and broad tires.

Mountain biking takes place off-road. It encompasses both competitive racing and purely recreational cycling. There are various off-road trails starting from the different resorts. You can start your tour right where you are, or you can go with a company up in the mountains and just take a ride downhill and enjoy the most breathtaking views of the island.

Below some companies with bicycling tours.

Federación Gran Canaria de Ciclismo	http://www.ciclismocanario.es
Free Motion - Bike & Outdoor	http://www.free-motion.net
Rocky Adventure	http://www.rockyadventure.com
Sportcanarias.com	http://www.sportcanarias.com
Biking and hiking in Gran Canaria	http://www.happy-biking.com

Golf

The never ending spring in Gran Canaria, with an annual temperature average of 21 C and the few raining days allows to practice golf every month in the year so why not combine Golf with vacation, sun and relaxation.

The island played a pioneering role with regard to golf in Spain, as the first golf course in the country was built at Escaleritas in 1891, followed by another in Bandamas in 1957. The first members of the Club Decano de España (known today as Real Club de Golf de Las Palmas) were members of the English colony on Gran Canaria, providing another example of the strong influence that Britain had on the birth of the island's tourism industry.

Despite the fact that Gran Canaria was a pioneer in including this sport, the development of the island's golfing infrastructure initially lagged behind that of other destinations, with most of the golf courses being of relatively recent construction, which means a clear advantage for the island as it has modern golf courses adapted to the most demanding golf players.

At present, there are six golf courses throughout Gran Canaria, although they are all situated within a maximum radius of 50 kilometres. Thus you can always try different courses within short distances.

Four new golf courses are currently under construction. The golf courses have been designed by the most prestigious international golf course designers and they all boast exceptional features. There is no doubt why national and international tournaments are held throughout the year.

With several thousand tourists, also playing Golf, together with the Islands local enthusiasts, you will often find a rather big pressure on many of the Golf courses, so it pays off to be in good time when you order your green fee. Among other things the Europe Tour has been held here several times.

Rock Climbing

If you have seen pictures of people perched on a small ledge thousands of feet up with no rope in sight and thought that perhaps rock climbing isn't for you then think again. You can learn the basics or improve your skills a few feet off of the ground.

We have companies offering rock climbing courses and holidays with trained instructors to suit all levels of climbers.

The delightful climate and an exceptional volcanic terrain with magnificent high peaks, are providing Gran Canaria with ideal conditions for practicing non-winter mountain sports. One of the most popular of these is rock climbing, which has an unexpected paradise of rocks and vertical cliffs waiting to be discovered in the island that by the way has generated some important school sites.

Volcanic eruptions and erosion created a paradise for all lovers of this sport, with rugged rock formations, rock needles, vertical cliffs, cracks, chimneys, gullies, crests, cauldrons, wedges, etc. everything a serious climber could wish for.

There are presently climbing sites all over the island. The most popular areas and climbing schools are found at the sites having good access possibilities and the best rock compositions such as Roque Nublo, which was the first climbing site to be developed on the island with 12 excellent routes and endless difficulties, El Palmés, El Toscón de Tejeda, Betancuria in Ayacata or Narices at the north face of Roque Bentayga. Climbing is restricted on this latter rock, because of its archaeological value.

Close to El Nublo there is also the rock circus of Ayacata, a sanctuary of traditional climbing with the largest number of classical routes of different lengths and degrees, scattered in the area or Tamada an ancient mountain massif with vertical cliffs in the northwest rising over the sea to an altitude of over 1000 m.

On its upper lave flows, you can find the sites of Lomo Caraballo, Supernova, la Perfumería and El Gulich, with its famous Emiliano

Zapata route, which made this area the sports climbing capital of Gran Canaria. Other areas known as La Librería, La Candelilla, El Frontón del GEC and El Montañón. Somewhat further away, El Pino and El Aserrador, offer the highest routes on basalt conglomerate walls on the island.

Other fascinating climbing sites such as a former climbing school, Costa Ayala, Bañaderos, sea cliffs located few kilometres from Las Palmas, along the northern motorway GC2, and Las Meleguinas, next to the bridge of the same name, in the borough of Santa Brígida.

The leading site for sports and boulder climbing in the south, La Sorrueda very near Santa Lucia in the Tirajana gulley, together with the southern gullies of Ayagaures and Berriel Fatagonia are the sites most attracted to climbers.

With the exception of a few publicly owned places, sites of special ecological sensitivity or military terrains, climbing is allowed everywhere. This makes it important for all climbers to respect, preserve and in no way disturb the natural environment and habitats of those areas, where they practice their sport.

Sports climbing requires certain regulative documents for your own security such as federation licence, insurance policy covering civil liability, accidents, etc.

We recommend you acquire more detailed and more up to date information about climbing sites, regulations, equipment, etc, from the Canary Island Federation of Mountaineering and Climbing before your departure to find all the details, or that you go with local climbers

Walking & Hiking

Walking and Hiking

Gran Canaria is the third largest island of the Archipelago of the Canary Islands and has a beautiful scenery which diversify the landscape for walking! With the arid but spectacular canyons of the South and the lush greener landscape of the North combined together makes Gran Canaria a walkers paradise!

In an attempt to create a more diversified tourism on the island, the Cabildo Insular de Gran Canaria (Regional Government) has invested in the recovery of the Caminos reales (royal paths) and reopened them to the public. These ancient paths, once the only means to get around in the interior of the island, centre on Cruz de Tejeda and radiate out from here to cover big parts of the island.

Some of the attractions you will see whilst trekking over the island include the magnificent Barranco de Fataga and Roque Nublo. From here you can see amazing views over the mountains of the Canary Islands including Snow capped Mount Teide in Tenerife!

Pozo De Las Nieves, is another which is the islands second highest peak at 6,317 ft, Pico De Las Nieves the islands highest point, The old Guanche cemetery, Montana Inagua, El Laurelillo ridge, Casas de Inagua ruins plus many more breathtaking views, wonderful canyons, little villages that lay hidden away, valleys and rocky peaks!

Almost 66,000 hectares of the island are protected land with rural parks, nature reserves, fully protected reserves and natural monuments, these old tracks giving access to most of this land. Some of these walks are newly built paths and there are some challenging ones with serious climbs, but there are also a series of relatively short and easy walks.

Be prepared
Walking or hiking is a great way of exploring less known, unspoilt landscapes and the dazzling beauty of the ancient Gran Canaria.

But conditions in the mountains can be very different from those on the coast, so make sure you are prepared for abruptly changing weather conditions and be equipped with good shoes, warm clothing, food, plenty of water, sun block and a good map. Also, we would advise you to never walk alone in these often quite deserted and rough areas in case of any mishap.

The Cabildo Insular de Gran Canaria publishes a series of leaflets, including maps, and although the information is in Spanish, basic details such as altitudes, length and duration of walks are clear.

There is also another useful book, called 'Gran Canaria: Rother Walking Guide', available in English from Amazon.co.uk

Jet & Water Skiing

There are many locations offering water-skiing, jet ski and also some parascending facilities. One of the place to go on Gran Canaria, is Puerto Rico.

The beaches near the town offer all the usual water sports, including jet-skiing, waterskiing and sailing; the crystal clear waters and abundant marine life ensure excellent views for scuba divers.

Parascending, jet skiing, water skiing, a trip on a speedboat and other active water sports are mostly offered in the main southern resorts. You will even find the ever popular banana boats, pedal boats and sea kayaks that are also available for hire and are a good way of getting out on the water with the kids!

Scuba Diving

Diving on Gran Canaria!

If you want to do a diving course whilst staying in Gran Canaria, it will not be a problem finding a fully certified diving school in any of the main coastal resorts as there are plenty!

Most of them offer courses for beginner and advanced courses for the more experienced divers, and most also let diving equipment.

The visibility is very good and the water temperature is about 22° C all year round. There are some great dives in the south including wreck and reefs. In the East there is the Marine Reserve called El Cabron which is one of only three in the Canary Islands and the diversity of fish and marine vegetation here is amazing! For the more experienced diver there are two old shipwrecks to explore in Pasito Blanco. Also northwest of Sardina and La Isleta there are some fantastic diving sites.

In the North there are also lots of wreck and reefs to see. Marine life you will see includes Angle Sharks (in the winter), Logger Head Turtles, Common Rays, Sting Rays, Bottle Nose Dolphin, Octopus, Cuttlefish, Morays, Barracuda, Trumpet Fish, Parrot fish, Groupers, Puffers, Sea Horses and many more reef fish.

Surfing & Bodyboarding

Surfing has a unique and often powerful appeal, which probably derives from an unusual confluence of elements: adrenaline, skill, and high paced manoeuvring are set against a naturally unpredictable backdrop? An organic environment that is, by turns, graceful and serene, violent and formidable.

Bodyboarding and surfing are best practised at the north. The best place to go is "El Alitalla" just north of Las Palmas between Las Palmas and Galdar. With constant on shore winds it is perfect conditions as waves can get up to five metres high!

There are several places you can hire the necessary equipment if you don't want to bring your own or if you don't have any!

There is also a few good places with good surfing and bodyboarding conditions along the east coast, around Vecindario, Arinaga (Pozo Izquierda) and in the south between Playa del Inglés and Maspalomas.

Here are also a couple of surf shops there if you're looking to buy a board or anything else appropriate.

Windsurfing

Steady winds, waves, sunshine and temperature all combine on Gran Canaria, making it a favourite destination for the world's surfers and wind surfers. So if you are looking for a place to travel to for your next windsurfing vacation, you have come to the right place.

Gran Canaria is the island that has the strongest and most consistent wind of all the seven islands. It blows about 80 % out of the whole year. Average wind is 3-5 bft from September through May and in the summer months 5 - 7 bft. In January and February we get most of our rain for the whole year.

For windsurfers it is actually no problem because these winter low pressures brings us nice south swells and normally storm. The south east side of Gran Canaria's coast line is where most of all the windsurfing take place. This is where the normal trade wind hits every day blowing north, north - east and east. Then pending on those angles the wind is stronger up or down the coast. In the summer months for example the trade wind is very north and there is only wind on the upper wind spots, whereas in winter months it blows more easterly and the wind line moves down the coast all the way past the south tip of the island, Maspalomas.

Sailing

The excellent international competitive performance by Canary Island yachtsmenis not a consequence of chance but due to Gran Canaria's optimum sailing conditions. This is attested to by the continued presence of so many yachts off the island's shore's enjoying the exceptional sailing environment in open, sun-drenched seas with steady prevailing winds.

Many international regattas either start of call at Gran Canaria and races are a commonplace event on the local sporting calendar, particularly for lateen, snipe and other class yachts as well as motor-boats. All equipment and kit necessary for yachting and sailing can be hired.

Gran Canaria has excellent marina facilities, its ports are frequently used by European yachtsmen as a take-off point for transatlantic crossings, or merely as a base for cruising the islands and enjoying the friendly warmth of the people and the climate.

This fact becomes indisputable if one takes account of the fact that the island has been the cradle of some thirty world champions in the various forms of sailing sports and of six Olympic gold medallists, namely José Luis Doreste, Luis Doreste, Roberto Molina, Patricia Guerra, Domingo Manrique de Lara and Fernando León. (Canary Island yachtsmen)

Almost any nautical sport is possible all the year round in Gran Canaria, with its mild climate, its varied coastline with over 236 km of coastline and almost 60 km of that being beaches, and the facilities offered in the many marinas.

These activities include sailing, waterskiing, surfing, windsurfing, bodyboarding, kitesurfing, deep sea fishing, parascending, jet and water skiing, shipwrecks and marine reservations for diving and sailing or the simple enjoyment of the sea.

The water temperature (which varies between 18ºC in winter and 22ºC during the rest of the year), the harbour infrastructure for yachting and the optimal sea and wind conditions make this island the ideal place for practicing sailing and other water sports all year round. In fact, water sports is the most important leisure activity on offer on the island.

Winds that are ideal for sailing, sea currents that attract large schools of fish to the proximity of the coast and the exquisite sea bottom are the natural conditions that have created one uninterrupted sporting season on Gran Canaria, while, in the rest of Europe, all activities related to the sea come to a complete standstill in winter.

Federación Insular de Vela de Gran Canaria
Muelle Deportivo

Las Palmas de Gran Canaria
Tel. 928 29 15 67

Real Club Victoria
Paseo de Las Canteras 4
Las Palmas de Gran Canaria
Tel. 928 46 06 30

Real Club Náutico de Gran Canaria
León y Castillo 308
Las Palmas de Gran Canaria
Tel. 928 23 45 66

Big-Game Fishing

If you enjoy Deep-sea fishing and Big-Game Fishing, then Gran Canaria is the place to come especially during the main season from May to September. All of the main resorts in Gran Canaria have several companies that offer deep-sea fishing, although the best places to set out from are in Puerto Rico, Pasito Blanco and Puerto de Mogán.

The best area for deep sea fishing, both in terms of the quantity of fish and the variety of species, lies between the Point at Maspalomas to the Point of "El Descojonado" (La Aldea de San Nicolas).

Whether you are a regular fisherman or someone that wants to catch your first bite. All ages will love the fishing here in Gran Canaria. With the calm ocean it really is a lovely day out. Be sure to take your sun cream and hat though, otherwise you may come back catching more than you bargained for - sunburn!!

Some excursion's starting as early as 08.30 hour. They range from 4 hours to 7 hours, so you will have part of the day still do to more exploring afterwards!!

Conditions in Gran Canaria are perfect all year round for fishing with water temperatures of 19°C in winter and 26°C in summer and a depth of up to 3.000 m around the island make Gran Canaria ideal for deep-sea fishing.

Marlin: Refers to different species with the common characteristic of an upper jaw ending in a long snout. These species are found in Canary Island waters, especially from May to November.

Blue Marlin: Gran Canaria is one of the places where the largest of these species can be caught. Regular catches of Blue Marlin range from 150 - 225 kg with last year's record standing at 360 kg.

White Marlin: Present in Gran Canaria throughout the summer.

Atlantic Spearfish: The Island holds the absolute world record for this marlin species.

Swordfish: The usual size of the species in island waters is 2.5 m. weighing in at over 84 kg.

Tuna: The Canary Island archipelago is in the middle of one of the most important tuna migration routes of the Atlantic. They pass Gran Canaria, especially the southern and north-western coast of the island, in the middle of spring, early summer, and from the start of autumn until winter arrives. The most common species are:

White tuna: The island holds several world records for this species, weighing in at over 30 kg.

Blue fin tuna: It is less common, but large individuals have been caught in excess of 366 kg.

Big-eye tuna: Gran Canaria is the world leader in this fish, with several world records in excess of 160 kg.

Skipjack tuna: It is particularly plentiful in Canary Island waters.

Yellow fin tuna: This species can also be caught in island waters.

Atlantic bonito: in abundance from March to July.

Dorado, Wahoo, Sharks and Hammerhead species, of interest to both amateur and professional fishermen, are to be found at no great distance from the shore; international championships are frequently held in these waters and to date 75 world records have been obtained. The broad range of professionally-organized fishing trips for both groups and individual delights those who come to Gran Canaria for fishing.

There's a good choice of companies offering deep-sea & big game fishing from Puerto Rico, Puerto de Mogán and also from the other harbours on the Island.

Shopping
Shopping in Gran Canaria
In all the Gran Canarian cities you will find a numerous and varied presence of shops in which you will be able to by all kind of products. Shopping in Gran Canaria remains a personal, rather than impersonal, experience. The majority of Spanish stores are small family run affairs.

The Gran Canarian often don't seem to believe in queuing and people often push and shove their way to the front. Shop assistants will not always serve customers in order; so if it is your turn - speak up! The last person in line is called "la ultima," and you may ask or be asked who is "La Ultima".

Some foreigners complain that Gran Canarian service people can be surly, but we have found the great majority of them to be friendly and pleasant.

One of the biggest attractions of shopping on the island is undeniably the low duties that are applied to certain imported goods, which means that one can find a series of products at prices that are between 10 and 30 percent lower than in the rest of the European territory.

Thus, one will find very competitive prices on the island for perfumes, cosmetics, tobacco, alcohol and, to a lesser extent, electronic apparatus and motor vehicles.

Gran Canaria have a lot of shopping streets. One of the best known in Las Palmas is the street Calle Mayor de Triana.

This street is a pedestrian zone and you can find all kinds of shops, cafés and restaurants here. Together with Vegueta this is one of the oldest districts in Las Palmas, and there are plenty of old buildings and beautiful architecture here.

Check out the shop of Zara. Housed in a beautiful building with a patio and traditional canarian balconies made of wood, all inside the shop. The Avenida Mesa y López is the main shopping street of Las Palmas. It stretches almost from Las Canteras in the west of the city to Playa Alcaravaneras in the east.

Here you can find many of the more exclusive and upper class shops of the city. But also plenty of other shops. The national shoppingcentre El Corte Inglés has two big buildings here with plenty of floors filled with all kinds of things.

About commerce
Gran Canaria has a long commercial tradition thanks to the activity of its strategic port, which was a free port until the accession of Spain to the EU. Through this port, the island has been supplied with the most diverse goods from the respective continents, including goods that have been difficult to find in other parts of the European continent.

In addition, Gran Canarias status as a tourist destination has placed the island in a very privileged position from a commercial point of view. Commerce has reached a high level of development on the island, being based mainly on a potential market of almost 4.5 million people, including the resident population, tourists and visitors.

Opening Hours:
Some bigger shops and stores may be closed on Sundays but the general opening hours are 10.00 - 20.00, with a few taking the customary siesta between 13.30 and 16.30..

Supermarkets are usually open between 10.00 - 22.00, although in the tourist resorts they might be open from 08.00 - 23.00 or 24.00

Shoppingcentre

If you like shopping, you're going to love Gran Canaria!
The big centres on the Gran Canaria provides a multitude of possibilities and provides pleasant satisfaction for the modern consumer.

A Duty Free mecca, your electrical goods, cigarettes, wines, beers and spirits, leather wear and designer clothes are all available at discounted prices.

Everything is more expensive in the south than in the north where there are not so many tourists. If you want to shop you should go to one of the big shopping malls. The closest to the south is Atlantico in Vecindario, close to the airport. Here you can find a great variety of shops, restaurants, bars and cinemas.

In Las Palmas you find the big Las Arenas right next to the Alfredo Kraus Auditorium on Las Canteras. And on the other side of the city, near the harbour, you find the newer El Muelle that also have discos. The street Mesa y Lopez is famous for it's shops and shopping malls, and of course there is the big shopping street Calle Mayor de Triana in the south of Las Palmas. About five minutes drive from Las Palmas you find the big 7 Palmas and El Corte Inglés right next to each other.

If you are interested in local crafts, clothes or food you should go to one of the markets that are held every week in many cities. For those who live in Playa del Ingles and Maspalomas it can often be better to shop in San Fernando, that lies close to the highway north of Maspalomas. This is the place where many locals live, and the prices are lower here.

Some bigger shops and stores may be closed on Sundays in but the general opening hours are 10.00 - 20.00, with a few taking the customary siesta between 13.30 and 16.30..

Supermarkets are usually open between 10.00 - 22.00, although in the tourist resorts they might be open from 08.00 - 23.00 or 24.00

There are ATMs (automated cash machines) all over the resorts and, as in other countries, guard your PIN number.

When using your credit cards in the tourist resorts, again guard your number if the store is using the new system, or ensure that the payment slip is correctly filled in before you sign it.

Below some of the biggest shopping centres on Gran Canaria.

Centro Comercial in Las Palmas

El Corte Inglés
Avenida Mesa y López 18

35007 Las Palmas

Tel. 928 26 30 00

El Corte Inglés have two big buildings on Calle Mesa y Lopez.

They have two high street stores in Las Palmas, one in Mesa y López, and one in 7 Palmas. They have nearly everything you need, as well as a lot of staff that help you find what you need. About five minutes drive from Las Palmas you find another El Corte Inglés and the big 7 palmas right next to each other.

Centro Comercial El Muelle

Muelle de Santa Catalina
Las Palmas de Gran Canaria

Tel. 928 32 75 27

Business hours: 10.00 - 22.00

On of the newest shopping centres on Gran Canaria is the ICSC (International Council of Shopping Centres) named "El Muelle" who is located in the Capital of Gran Canaria, Las Palmas not far from the famous Santa Catalina Park. This is one of the best shopping centres in Europe.

The centre has 60 shops, 30 restaurants, cafés, bars and an open air disco, approximately 5000 m2 in size. Eleven cinemas can also be found there, and there's a bowling alley with 14 lanes.

Centro Comercial Siete Palmas

Avenida Pintor Felo Monzón

35013 Las Palmas

Tel. 928 42 41 68

Fax. 928 42 41 68

Business hours: 10.00 - 22.00

Restaurants keep open until 03.00 h.

This is a fairly new area of Las Palmas, integrating residential areas and great shopping. Here you find Media Markt, which is the largest electronics mega store in the islands. You also find Zara, Cortefiel, hair dressers and a nice café at the bottom floor. Tip: In the garage you can have your car washed and pressed while you go shopping. It also has a cinema and 10 pin bowling.

Centro Commercial Las Arenas

Ctra. del Rincón

35010 Las Palmas

Tel. 928 49 49 90

Business hours: 10.00 - 22.00

This shopping centre is situated close to Paseo de las Canteras and next to the Alfredo Krauss auditorium. It offers a host of different retail outlets, from restaurants (including McDonalds) and bars to a huge supermarket (Carrefour), as well as shops selling clothes (Zara, Mango etc.), music, computer products, children's goods, perfumes and more. Within the complex you'll also find a six-screen cinema, an outdoor terrace and a play area for children. There is a large, free car park with outdoor and covered areas. Its pyramid shape makes it visible from afar and it has become a commercial symbol of the city. Don't forget to stroll down the beach afterwards!

La Ballena

Ctra.gral. Norte, 112

35013 Las Palmas

Tel. 928 41 14 55

This was the first mall of Las Palmas, constructed in the late 80´s. They have all the shops that you need, as well as a cinema complex.

Centro Comercial in Telde

Hipermercado Alcampo

Autovía GC-1 Km 8

35212 Telde

Tel. 928 13 40 00

Business hours: 09.00 - 22.00

This hyper-market belongs to the international group Auchan and can be found just off the motorway that joins Las Palmas to the south of the island. Its size makes it easily visible from the motorway and it has a large, free, supervised parking area at the front.

As well as all the usual supermarket goods, you can also buy jewellery, electronic goods, music, furniture, etc. There are also other businesses located within the complex, like a photography shop, a tobacconist, a newsagent, clothes shops, shoe shops, and banks.

Leroy Merlin
Parque Comercial La Mareta
Autovía Gran Canaria, 1, Km. 8
35200 Telde
Tel. 928 70 76 00
Fax. 928 70 66 16
Business hours: 10.00 - 22.00

Leroy Merlin practices the magic of local adaptation. The company, one of Europe's largest home-improvement retailers, operates stores who are designed to meet the different home-improvement needs of each country. Besides the usual DIY products, Leroy Merlin's stores carry building materials, sanitary equipment, and decorative items.

Makro

Autovía GC-1 Km 8

35200 Telde

Tel. 928 70 37 70

Fax. 928 70 37 61

Opening hours:

Monday - Saturday 09.00 - 21.00

Makro is a wholesaler offering a food and non-food product mix to its registered card-holding customers in a national network of cash and carrys. It is a unique out of town food and non-food concept, offering a wholesale solution to professional business needs.
This warehouse demands a card from an independent company.

Centro Comercial in Vecindario

Centro Comercial Atlántico

C/ Adargoma, Vecindario

35110 Santa Lucía de Tirajana

Tel. 928 79 40 74

Opening hours: 09.00 - 03.00

Business hours: 10.00 - 22.00

Further down south along the highway, in Vecindario which is only 15 minutes from Maspalomas. Has new names including Zara, Jack & Jones, Vera Moda, Mango, a big **Carrefour Supermarket** and others. Its actually quite cheap and especially over the Christmas month. If you go to the Canary Islands to shop, which you really shouldn't, go there.

Latest fashion, music and DVD, home appliances, pets and more. Also has a cinema and few restaurants. A McDonalds is both inside the mall and one is outside.

Centro Comercial La Ciel
Avenida de Canarias 338, Vecindario
35110 Santa Lucía de Tirajana
Business hours: 09.00 - 22.00

Vecindario is one of the major commercial areas of the island. This is where the large shopping centres can be found (C.C. Atlántico, C.C. La Ciel, C.C. Avenida de Canarias). Fashion stores, large leisure centres (restaurants, cinemas, terrace bars...), large supermarkets, etc, can all be found within Vecindario.

Centro Comercial in Playa del Inglés, Maspalomas and Meloneras

Centro Comercial Varadero

C/ Mar Mediterráneo

35100 Meloneras

Tel. 928 14 11 77

Fax. 928 14 09 70

Business hours: 10.00 - 22.00

The shopping centre Varadero in Meloneras. The shopping centre is one of the best visited centres in the south of Gran Canaria.

Yumbo

Avd. de E.E.U.U.

35100 Playa del Inglès

Tel. 928 76 67 68

Opening hours: 24 h.

Business hours: 10.00 - 22.00

The C.C.YUMBO makes shopping pleasure become a holiday attraction. Open architecture, spacious green areas, 200 shops and restaurants have a magnetic attraction for visitors from Playa del Inglés and Maspalomas. Enjoy your holiday time in the unique restaurants and bars of the YUMBO Center. You really deserve it!

Cita

Avd. de Francia

35100 Playa del Inglés

Tel. 928 76 28 43

Fax. 928 76 28 43

Opening hours: 24 h.

Business hours: 10.00 - 22.00

The CITA shopping centre is one of the oldest and best known shopping centres on Gran Canaria. Located in the centre of Playa del Inglés it is close to the beautiful dunes and the famous beach. About 200 shops and catering establishments are ready to serve and entertain a clientele from the whole world.

A "short" stop for shopping at the CITA can go on for 24 hours. Features like the children=s playground, a mini-golf course, amusement arcades and numerous cafés, bars, pubs and restaurants turn CITA into an international leisure centre.

Faro II

Avda. Touroperator

(Holland International -

Campo International)

35100 Maspalomas

Tel. 928 76 91 97

Fax. 928 76 88 77

Opening hours: 24 h.

Business hours: 10.00 - 22.00

Restaurants keep open until 24.00 h.

Pubs until 03.00 h.

In Faro 2 there is a mix of a modern Shopping Centre, the beauty of the architecture project, and the comfort to be in one of the most privileged areas of the island, 50 Kilometres away from Las Palmas, and surrounded by beautiful housing estates.

The proximity to a broad range of hotels and luxurious housing estates like Gran Hotel Costa Meloneras, IFA Hotel Faro Maspalomas, Hotel Playa Meloneras Palace, Riu Meloneras Palace, Massage centers, Health resorts, Spa centres, etc, turn Faro 2 into a perfect place for a high or medium-high standard of living clients who decide to buy in this complete and varied Shopping Centre.

C.C. Kasbah

Avd. de Tenerife

35100 Playa del Inglès

Tel. 928 76 22 38

Opening hours: 24 h.

Bars & disco open until 06.00 h.

Kasbah is a small but nice Shopping Centre and one of the main centres of Playa del Inglés for entertainment. Not too many shops but you can walk around.

It also boasts an outdoor dance floor with live music most evenings where you can waltz the night away (literally), and plenty of bars and restaurants. The Kasbah Centre is more for young people and the Plaza Shopping Centre is where you go to hear the latest international music. The Kasbah basically forms one big centre along with the Plaza and Metro Centres.

Plaza De Maspalomas
Avda. Italia, s/n - Playa del Inglés
35100 San Bartolomé de Tirajana
Tel. 928 77 87 71
Opening hours: 24 h.

The Plaza Shopping Centre has a large number of shops open during the day and is a lively nightlife spot. It is underground and the bars are arranged in a semi-circle around a central circle reached by escalators.

Good shopping in the Plaza center by day though, including a Visanta Centre and they have an excellent reputation in retailing electrical goods, offering a money back promise for the duration of your holiday if you're not satisfied with your purchase and give European guarantees. They're recommended to clients of major tour operators.

Centro Comercial Metro

Avda. Italia, s/n - Playa del Inglés

35100 San Bartolomé de Tirajana

Tel.

Opening hours: 24 h.

One of the best of a dozen or so centres in Playa del Ingles is probably the Metro Centre not that far from the north end of Playa del Inglés' beach (and where all the nightlife is). Really good choice of shops but the owners are expecting tourists so you don't always get the best price or deal, even if you are spoilt for choice.

Centro Comercial Gran Chaparral

Avda de Gran Canaria,

Playa del Ingles

Opening hours: 24 h.

Once known as "the English Centre", the Gran Chaparral now also very popular with the Dutch. It has a large range of British, Dutch and Scandinavian bars and restaurants, many of which show the football and the soaps. It could never be described as pretty but it is a good place to go for a good breakfast. There's also a couple of bike shops renting cycles and motorbikes.

Shopping Center Tropical

C/ Madrid 1, Playa del Inglés

35100 San Bartolomé de Tirajana

Tel. 928 77 35 14

Opening hours: 24 h.

The Tropical shopping centre by the main Playa del Ingles bus station has a good mix of shops, including a "Fundgrube" which sells perfumes and gifts, as well as restaurants. The advantage of the Tropical is the great view of the Playa del Ingles beach and Maspalomas Dunes from the restaurant terraces.

Centro Comercial Anexo II

Paseo Marítimo, Playa del Inglés

35100 San Bartolomé de Tirajana

Anexo II is located at the north end of Playa del Inglés and right on the beach front. All this is beach shops, restaurants and bars all by the beach. Anexo II is a very busy place by day and by night. The beach here goes on for 6 km and this is the only part with restaurants by it, as well as the only water sports being here too so very much the place to be for a brilliant beach & holiday atmosphere by night and by day.

Centro Comercial in San Fernando

Bellavista

Partera Leonorita, s/n (San Fernando)

35100 San Bartolomé de Tirajana

Tel. 928 77 63 89

This is the Canarian district and we recommend that you shop there instead of places like Yumbo and Cita. The prices vary but are usually lower than anywhere else. The difference can be up to 50%! Its worth it to take a look there. The merchants there will also not cheat on you, what you see is what you get and prices are always displayed. As well as the large, local supermarkets (Hyperdino in the Bellavista centre boasts the cheapest prices on Gran Canaria) there's a huge choice of every other type of shop also. Avenida de Galdar is a good street to look along and just in front of it there are two commercial centres aimed for residents rather than tourists.

San Fernando

Av. Tejeda, s/n - San Fernando

35100 San Bartolomé de Tirajana

Tel. 928 76 90 90

C. C. San Fernando, however, is interesting. A long time ago it was the major shopping area around here.

Centro Comercial in Puerto Rico

Centro Comercial Puerto Rico

Av. Tomás Roca Bosch - Puerto Rico

35130 Mogán

Tel. 928 56 07 32

This is situated in the centre of the resort and consists of three continuous phases. Whilst accesses are via steps, there are also wheelchair ramps.

The upper floor contains the majority of the restaurants, disco bars and clubs, while the ground floor houses shops, bars and banks. It is here that the larger supermarkets, Netto and Spar are situated, although many smaller ones are scattered around the resort and the other two centres Europa Centre and Agua de Perra as well as some small privately owned outlets.

On the lower ground you will find a small selection of shops, another large supermarket, a pharmacy and the Bureau de Change / Tourist Office, where you can pick up information on tours, etc.. Watch out also for the various kiosks and stands around the resort which give discounts on all kinds of entertainment.

Taxfree

Canary Islands have been duty-free since 1852 with a low duty and low VAT. and low customs duties. That's is why there is a very small difference on prices in normal shops and in the airport.

Almost everything can be bought cheaper in the shops here, than what you have to pay in the airport or on the plane. Think about is, before you buy or order.

On the south side of the Island, the vacation resorts have their own malls. Most are built because of the Tourists, and the prices are according to. It is therefore a good idea to notice what the goods costs in other shops. Often the goods can be acquired for half price in the smaller shops. Feel free to visit our advertisers under Shops.

(Remember - in many shops there are Siesta about 13.00 - 16.30)

Now it would be inexpedient to bring cigarettes and liquor here, as Gran Canaria is an EU member, but not is considered as an EU-country what duties are concerned. It is much cheaper down here. About customs the rules are the same whichever way you are travelling, that is you can bring the same quantity with you here, as you can bring home.

You have to watch yourself, if you travel via Andorra, and feel like buying duty-free there, as it is a "duty free" state. Then you are in big trouble! Andorra is not an EU member and it is only legal to buy 200 cigarettes and on litre of liquor, and bring to Spain. The border control between Andorra and Spain is very tough.

The Island has a sales tax (VAT) of 4.5% making it one of the cheapest destinations in Western Europe.

Custom rules:

(Persons under 17 years of age, cannot bring tobacco and spirits)

Spirits (> 22%):	1 litre
Dessert Wine (< 22%)	2 litre
Table wine:	2 litre
Coffee	500 gram or Coffee extract: 200 g.
Tee:	100 gram or Tee extract: 40 gram
Tobacco:	
- Cigarettes or	200 stk.
- Cigars or	50 stk.
- Cigarillos or	100 stk.
- Smoking tobacco	250 gram
Perfume:	50 cc/ml
Toilet water:	250 cc/ml.

Beside this you can bring duty-free goods to an total of 145 £ per person

Markets

Almost every city has their own market, many of them are on Sundays but there are also other markets every day of the week. Here you can find all the traditional meals, local handcrafts, clothes and all kinds of things. And the best is that it's much cheaper to buy it here than in any other places.

The most popular is the Sunday market in Teror, where locals from all over the island come and there are not so many tourists here. If you want to go to this city, go on a Sunday so you can see the market too. If you're not going to Teror there are also markets in places like Mogán, Puerto de Mogán, Arguineguín and Telde in the south. See calendar below.

On the Markets you can buy what ever you want, but rest assure that 98% of what you see from electronics and leather, is pirated editions. And it often is impossible to notice the difference, if you don't have the original item besides you.

In the big centres in Puerto Rico, Playa del Ingles and Maspalomas, it is often Indian who owns the shops, you have to remember to haggle the prise, as you often can reduce the prise to half of where they started.

Don't bring more money than what is necessary, or keep an eye on your values, because there are much people - and not everyone is honest.

Don't be cheated.

Electronics

When buying electronics (video cameras, digital cameras, Mobil telephones and computer games) we recommend the shops named VISANTA. Here they are honest and tell you about the guarantee, you can take out on the products. Remember to get an receipt and and remember to have the guarantee ticket stamped. - and hide both items. - Visit their home-page and and compare product and prise from home. www.visanta.es

Below the Markets on Gran Canaria

Agüimes

Every Thursday 08.00 - 14.00 next to the municipal swimming pool

Arguineguín

Every Tuesday 08.00 - 14.00 at the market square

Every Thursday 08.00 - 14.00 in the Ancora Centre

The Islands biggest market takes place every Tuesday 08.00 - 14.00, where it is possible to buy almost everything. Also pirated editions. You should control the marking to be sure. It is a good idea to haggle about the prices, as it often is possible to buy things for under half price of where it started. Don't bring more money than you find necessary - or keep an eye on your values. There's a lot of people here, and not everyone is that honest.

Arucas

Market every Saturdy from 08.00 - 14.00 on C/ Alcalde Codorniú Rodríguez y Fernando Caubín Ponce

Gáldar

Every Thursday 08.00 - 14.00 on the market place - Plaza de Santiago

Las Palmas

Every Sunday 08.00 - 14.00 on the top floor of the bus terminal by the San Telmo Park

Moya

Every Sunday there´s a market on Estación de Guaguas from 08.00 - 14.00

Puerto de Mogán

Every Friday 08.00 - 14.00 by the harbour where you can buy almost everything, also pirated editions, so please control the marking to be sure. (You could take the ferry from Arguineguín - Anfi or Puerto Rico and enjoy the beautiful sail)

San Bartolomé de Tirajana

Every Sunday 09.00 - 14.00 there's a market on the marketplace "Mercatunte"

San Fernando

Every Wednesday and Saturday 08.00 - 14.00 by the Market Hall opposite the fire station.

San Mateo

Every Saturday: 07.00 - 19.00
Every Sunday: 07.00 - 14.00

Real Canarian market in the market halls where you can buy almost everything,of course many local goods, but also pirated editions so control the labels to be sure.

Folk music and dans on the market place.

Santa Brigida

Every Saturday 08.00 - 20.00

Every Sunday 08.00 - 20.00

Santa Lucia

Every Sunday there's a market by the Town Hall in Santa Lucia from 09.00 - 14.00.

Santa María de Guía

Every Tuesday and Sunday there's a market in Santa María de Guía close by the City Hall from 08.30 - 13.00.

Telde

Every Saturday 08.00 - 14.00 next to the bus station

Teror

Here in Teror we find the local market at the square by the church, arranged every Sunday 8.00 - 14.00, and where you can find a richly choice of goods you can't find in the shops or on the markets in the South of the Island.

Valleseco

Mercadillo Municipal local market every Sunday 08.00 - 14.00

Valsequillo

Every Sunday there´s a market on Isla de La Gomera - 8.00 - 14.00

Vecindario

Every Monday 08.00 - 14.00 canarian market in the market building

Every Wednesday 08.00 - 14.00 common market in the same building

In Vecindario there's a market every Monday and Wednesday at 08.00 - 14.00. This and the fact, that the City has a long Main Street filled with shops, and the big Atlántico Centre, makes Wednesday the best Day to visit the Town. The prices here are among the cheapest on the Island.

Service Area

Hotel Booking

Hotels on Gran Canaria

On Gran Canaria you will find a lot of hotels, apartments and lodging opportunities.

When was the last time you treated yourself to an extravagant holiday?

Gran Canaria is unconditionally one of the most sun-safe places among the close winter destinations.

Service fit for royalty is what guests can expect when they stay at hotels on Gran Canaria. Gran Canarias hotels offer five-star amenities and world class service at reasonable rates. Hotels on Gran Canaria provide luxurious accommodation through rooms equipped with comfortable beds, telephone, personal safe, air-conditioning, spacious bathrooms, mini bar and satellite television.

Gran Canaria Island hotels and resorts reservation guide - the definitive guide to Gran Canaria Island accommodation.

The Gran Canaria Island hotels and resorts guide provides a brief summary, customer ratings and reviews for hotels or resorts.

For a quick summary see the list of hotels and resorts in Gran Canaria Island. For detailed hotel information or to reserve a hotel or resort in Gran Canaria Island, please select a hotel or resort and let hotelsguiden.com be your Gran Canaria Island travel agent.

Whatever type of accommodation you require on your holiday in Gran Canaria you will find it here.

For hotels in Gran Canaria or apartments in Gran Canaria you don't have to look further.

Baby - Services

Unique family-service.

The professional and reliable pram- and pushchair hire service. For the security of your child and also for your perfect family holiday we offer indispensable, special baby and children journey accessories for parents.

You can choose between especially sure all-terrain and beach fit pushchairs and prams and also handcarts, travel cots and high chairs and you can easily hire this products online directly on these pages. Delivery in all hotels and villas. - All items are top quality products and in perfect condition..

Silvias Buggyservice - the big hire service in Europe - guarantees a perfect service in cooperation with big tour operators, airlines and many travel agencies (to very favourable conditions) since 1997..
We deliver our products directly to your vacation hotel / finca / villa of the family-friendly vacation areas mentioned above and collect them there again - without surcharge.
Silvias Buggyservice currently operates in many family-friendly vacation areas exactly where you need it. This is really simple and also very comfortable for you. It couldn't be easier!.

Weather

The Canaries enjoy worldwide fame, gained because of its mild climate, one of the best in the whole world. Gran Canarias weather is mild, with pleasant temperatures, rarely too high and almost always constant. And the climate is probably the most powerful element to attract millions of tourists and residents every year.

A sub-tropical oceanic climate which is constant almost the whole year round, but with a great difference between the islands and even between the North and the South of one single island. From the driest islands Fuerteventura and Lanzarote, with only 150 - 200 mm rain a year, the old volcano the Teide with most of the months snow on the top to the green humid island La Palma with green forests and the sand dunes on Gran Canaria which looks like the Sahara.

The weather is almost constant sunshine all year round with passing clouds. If you're very unlucky it will rain, ranging from light drizzle to a torrential downpour, but this is rare. It's slightly cloudier in October, some rain in November and December and a bit colder in January and February. As a rule, you can say that the sun shines on more than 300 days a year! If it is raining, the rain comes in short bursts of heavy showers, 20, 30 minutes and that's it.

As with other Canary Islands, the climate in the north of Gran Canaria often differs from the south, most temperatures are given from Las Palmas - expect it to be around 5°C cooler in the north. The warm and dry climate, mainly at the South side of the islands, is comfortable in the winter and mostly between 22ºC and 29ºC. This makes the Canaries very attractive for sun vacations in the summer months between 26ºC and 28ºC, often exceeding 30°C, and in the winter months between 22ºC and 24ºC.

Many people who are suffering from arthritis or rheumatism are getting a new life here, thanks to the gentle and constantly warm climate.

Sometimes, you can see snow in the highest peaks, and just a few kilometres away you will get both tropical temperatures and extreme cold.

Accommodation

Apartments

Luxurious Gran Canaria apartments and self-catering apartments and other Gran Canaria accommodations offer calm and refuge to visitors seeking the ultimate tropical island escape.

With the unbeatable Mediterranean climate of the Canary Islands, holiday rentals on Gran Canaria can be found within easy distance of a

choice of glorious sandy beaches, and the bustling city of Las Palmas means you can explore the native architecture and exploit the shops of this lively Canary Island.

Apartment rentals on Gran Canaria are becoming increasingly popular and can be rented on a weekly basis.

Offering inexpensive and well placed accommodation, Gran Canaria is home to more than 1000 apartments which are available for rental around the year.

Holiday homes on Gran Canaria are available to suit every requirement of comfort and convenience, and a holiday apartment on Gran Canaria with 1 bedroom would be the perfect destination for a romantic break for two, giving you complete freedom to unwind in your own luxury holiday accommodation.

An apartment on Gran Canaria with a sweeping view of the blue ocean will take care of that. Your holiday apartment on the Canary Islands will exceed all your expectations, if you choose to rent an apartment on Gran Canaria with a pool - an idyllic and luxurious base from where you can discover all the richness and beauty of this breathtaking Island.

Bungalows

Luxurious holiday bungalows on Gran Canaria being another option that might better suit the requirements of your family.

With the unbeatable Mediterranean climate of the Canary Islands, holiday rentals on Gran Canaria can be found within easy distance of a choice of glorious sandy beaches, and the bustling city of Las Palmas means you can explore the native architecture and exploit the shops of this lively Canary Island.

Bungalow rentals on Gran Canaria are becoming increasingly popular and can be rented on a weekly basis. Offering inexpensive and well placed accommodation.

Holiday homes on Gran Canaria are available to suit every requirement of comfort and convenience, and an accommodation on Gran Canaria is ideal for a family vacation where the opportunities for leisure and recreation cater for people of all ages, with beach games for the youngsters, sunbathing and water sport, coach trips through the mountains or to coffee plantations and vineyards, even the prospect of a golfing holiday, bungalows on Gran Canaria can deliver whatever you want from your vacation.

A bungalow on Gran Canaria with a sweeping view of the blue ocean will take care of that.

Your holiday bungalows on the Canary Islands will exceed all your expectations, and if you choose to rent a bungalow on Gran Canaria with a pool - you'll have an idyllic and luxurious base from where you can discover all the richness and beauty of this breathtaking Island.

Camping

Gran Canaria also have some very good campsites.
For instance Camping Temisas in Aguimes, Camping Pasito Blanco in Maspalomas and Camping El Pinillo i Arguineguín!

In all tree you can rent space for your Motor Home (RV), Caravan or Tents!! Pets are allowed in the plots. It is easily accessible for bigger vehicles. Surrounded by trees and other plant life, it is beautifully situated for those of you who like the outdoor way of living!

Facilities included for all: Restaurant, Bar, Supermarket and swimming pool. There are warm water showers, toilets, laundry and wash basins. Electricity and Gas are both available too!

Areas and recreational areas where to stay in the nature, and where there are room for Auto campers and Caravans.

Área de acampada Llano del Salado Side road to el cruce de los Llanos de la Pez Area covering about 500 m² with 10 places	Área de acampada Corral de los Juncos Ctra. Cruz de los Llanos - Ayacata Area covering about 20.000 m² with 300 places
Albergue Albergue de Montaña de Tejeda Tomás Arroyo Cardoso - Tejeda Area covering about 2000 m² with 34 places and the only one from above mentioned you can get to by means of Public Transportation.	Campamento Cortijo de Huertas Ctra. Cruz de los Llanos - Ayacata Area covering about 20.000 m² with 60 places.
Centro de Visitantes Parque Arqueológico del Bentayga Side road to Ctra. al Roque Area covering about 160 m² with 25 places.	Centro de Visitantes Parque Rural del Nublo Ctra. Cruz de Tejeda a Los Pechos

Área recreativa Llanos de la Pez Ctra. Cruz de los Llanos - Ayacata Area covering about 30.000 m² with 500 places	Área recreativa Presa Cueva de las Niñas Ctra. Ayacata - Presa de las Niñas Area covering about 15.000 m² with 100 places

Villas

Luxurious holiday villas on Gran Canaria being another option that might better suit the requirements of your family.

With the unbeatable Mediterranean climate of the Canary Islands, holiday rentals on Gran Canaria can be found within easy distance of a choice of glorious sandy beaches, and the bustling city of Las Palmas means you can explore the native architecture and exploit the shops of this lively Canary Island.

Villa rentals on Gran Canaria are becoming increasingly popular and can be rented on a weekly basis. Offering inexpensive and well placed accommodation. Holiday homes on Gran Canaria are available to suit every requirement of comfort and convenience, and an accommodation on Gran Canaria is ideal for a family vacation where the opportunities for leisure and recreation cater for people of all ages, with beach games for the youngsters, sunbathing and water sport, coach trips through the mountains or to coffee plantations and vineyards, even the prospect of a golfing holiday, villas on Gran Canaria can deliver whatever you want from your vacation.

A villa on Gran Canaria with a sweeping view of the blue ocean will take care of that.

Your holiday villas on the Canary Islands will exceed all your expectations, and if you choose to rent a villa on Gran Canaria with a pool - you'll have an idyllic and luxurious base from where you can discover all the richness and beauty of this breathtaking Island.

Hostels

Gran Canaria has different hostels around the island. Two of them are based in the capital of the island, Las Palmas; Hostal Alcaravaneras and Falow Hostel.

Hostal Alcaravaneras is located in Las Palmas, just about 50 m from the beach, and you will find everything just a few minutes away, as

the hostel is very close to the shopping area of Las Palmas. The hostel has all the facilities you will need for your holiday including; Safe Box availability, Towels, Linen, Free Internet Access, 24 hour Television room, 24 hour reception, No curfew and No Lockout! It is clean and the staff are friendly.

Falow Hostel is located in Las Palmas, only 70 m from Alcaravaneras beach, and with just a 10 minute walk to Las Canteras beach. By the way Las Canteras beach is considered one of the best beaches on the island!

Also within close walking distance of the hostels is the shopping area of Las Palmas, where you will find all sorts of shops, cafes, bars and restaurants.

The hostel has double, twin and single rooms, with or without toilet. For standard rooms you will find a toilet and shower on each floor. The facilities include; Towels, Linen, Luggage storage. No curfew and no lockout!

It is a clean and quite hostel, with a friendly staff.

Rural Hotels

Rural accommodation (casa rural) are also equally desirable around Gran Canaria and are never far from local shops and eateries.

With the unbeatable Mediterranean climate of the Canary Islands, rural accommodation on Gran Canaria can be found within easy distance of a choice of glorious sandy beaches and the bustling city of Las Palmas. That means you can explore the native architecture and exploit the shops of this lively metropolis of the Canary Island

Rural accommodation rentals on Gran Canaria are becoming increasingly popular and can be rented on a weekly or monthly basis. Offering inexpensive and well placed accommodation, Rural accommodations on Gran Canaria are available to suit every requirement of comfort and convenience, and rural accommodation on Gran Canaria is ideal for a family vacation where the opportunities for leisure and recreation cater for people of all ages, with beach games for the youngsters, sunbathing and water sport, coach trips through the mountains or to coffee plantations and vineyards, even the prospect of a golfing holiday - rural accommodation on Gran Canaria can deliver whatever you want from your vacation.

Rural accommodation on Gran Canaria with a sweeping view of the blue ocean or the mountains will take care of that.

Your rural accommodation on the Canary Islands will exceed all your expectations if you choose to rent an rural house on Gran Canaria.

Private rentals

Private rentals on Gran Canaria self-catering apartments and other Gran Canaria accommodations.

With the unbeatable Mediterranean climate of the Canary Islands, holiday rentals on Gran Canaria can be found within easy distance of a choice of glorious sandy beaches, and the bustling city of Las

Palmas means you can explore the native architecture and exploit the shops of this lively Canary Island.

Apartment rentals on Gran Canaria are becoming increasingly popular and can be rented on a monthly or yearly basis. Offering inexpensive and well placed apartments, duplex, bungalows or villas Gran Canaria is home to many thousand apartments which are available for rental year-round.

Holiday or living homes on Gran Canaria are available to suit every requirement of comfort and convenience, and a holiday apartment on Gran Canaria with 1, 2 or 3 bedroom would be the perfect destination for families who want to work, live or just are on vacation down here.

An apartment on Gran Canaria with a sweeping view of the blue ocean will take care of that.

Your holiday apartment on the Canary Islands will exceed all your expectations, and if you choose to rent an apartment on Gran Canaria with a pool - you'll get an idyllic and luxurious base from where you can discover all the richness and beauty of this breathtaking Island.

Real Estate

Real Estate - Residences for sale & hire

Gran Canarian property can be a very good opportunity for investment!

Buying property down here is ideal, if you are looking for a laid back and relaxing lifestyle on Gran Canaria which has an excellent climate throughout the year.

If you are an investor looking to buy property to rent out, then these years seem to be the best for buying and most popular with the holiday makers due to the properties versatility.

Transport

Airport

Las Palmas Airport is situated in Gando, approximately in the middle of the East coast.

Gran Canaria Airport is about 18 km. from the Islands main town of Las Palmas de Gran Canaria and a taxi into the City will cost about 25 €.

The present Airport is built in 1993, and you drive 20 minutes to reach Las Palmas, 30 minutes to Playa del Ingles and about 45 minutes to Puerto Rico.

When you arrive at Gran Canaria airport you will collect your luggage from one of three different zones. Zone A is for all passengers travelling from within the EU, Zone B is for all other International traffic and Zone C is for all Inter Canary Island flights.

Direct plane to and from Madrid takes a little more than 2 hours.

All Islands has got an airport for National and International flights, except La Gomera, to which you can only fly from Tenerife and Las Palmas Gran Canaria with Binter Canarias.

Bus

Local bus
Local bus transportation is functioning well all over the Island. Bus services provide the cheapest way of getting around the island and cover a large proportion of its significant destinations as well as some of the smaller villages. Buses are easily identified by their green and

blue colour and all are clearly marked with their service number and destination. Frequent and reliable services run between Puerto Rico, Las Palmas, Playa del Inglés and Maspalomas.

On the southern part of the Island the busses are green and blue and are named Salcai Global. On the North side of the Island, they are blue and are named Utinsa Global.

You buy the ticket direct in the bus, when going into the bus, and notice, that the chauffer normally doesn't change bills. Therefore always remember coins to the bus.

Rent a Car

There are unbelievable much to experience and explore on Gran Canaria and it is very cheap to rent a car (from about 30 € a day). In this price is free kilometres and a traffic insurance, but no accident and person insurance.

Car hire transport companies are abundant around Gran Canaria and offer an extremely affordable way to explore the island. Many people choose to rent a car when visiting Gran Canaria, so that they have the freedom to travel when and where they wish.

When renting a car on Gran Canaria, drivers must be at least 21 years of age at some places up to 25 years of age. Small cars often offer the best value for money, although older cars can be particularly cheap. On Gran Canaria, cars must always drive on the right-hand side of the road.

If you want to rent a motorcycle, moped or scooter, they are normally let through the same shops, that let cars at the resort.

By parking, the blue colour on the street means, that you have to pay for the parking most of the day. Information's bout parking fees is on the parking meter. A yellow line means, that parking is prohibited.

Speed limits in Spain are as follows: 20 kph in residential areas, 50 kph in built-up areas, 90 kph in country roads, 100 kph in dual carriageways, 120 kph on motorways, 80 kph for cars towing a trailer on divided highways and 70 kph on other roads.

The use of safety belt is obligatory - also on the back seat. Unlawful parked cars is removed by the police and a considerable fine is unavoidable. As of May 1. 2004 there is passed a new traffic law that is sharpening the security measures on the roads.

It includes for instant the use of Internet, TV, Video and DVD - and of course the hand held telephone & drivers smoking. Only GPS and hands free Mobil-installation is permitted when driving. Installations in the car, with the purpose of disclosing speed control is also forbidden, and it is not permitted to signal other motorists about a traffic control.

In the future there must be 2 warning triangles in the car. Children under 12 Years of age, measuring below 1,5 meter have to be kept in children seats/chairs.

Reflex waist coats - and now it's time to buy at least one reflex waist coat, to use if you have to get out of the car during a stop or traffic accident.

From. July 1, 2004 there webcams are placed in order to supervise the Traffic in Las Palmas activated by built in radar control, so you better keep the speed limits, if you don't want the vacation to be too expensive.

From the 10. August 2005 the fines rise for driving without the safety belt and if you are talking Mobil, while driving, if it isn't a hands free. Payment at once, so remember to have some cash in the pocket.

Taxi

Metered taxis are readily available across the island and are generally cheap, although unscrupulous taxi drivers may try to rip off unwitting tourists by claiming not to have any change for large bills. You may wish to approach your hotel to book a taxi for you, since hotels generally have arrangements with

local drivers/companies or can at least recommend a reputable service to you. There are taxis available at the airport, and you will find the Gran Canaria airport taxis on a rank outside of each of the three main arrival zones. On your return to the airport the taxi drivers will drop you off outside the departures hall.

They are white and with a different colour on the roof depends of which city the taxies are from. Other signs that might help you recognize a taxi are the letters SP (meaning 'Servicio Público') and a green light on top or in the front windscreen. At certain times of day, (for example 19.00 - 22.00), is it impossible to go for 30 seconds without passing an available taxi. Other times (e.g.. after midnight) you might have to walk to a main road or taxi rank, but you still won't have to wait long.

Taxi drivers are very proud of their cars, which are always spotless. They are less likely to pick you up if you are wearing fetish gear and won't take you at all if you're covered in sand.

This is the quickest but most expensive option. Costs vary according to your final destination.

If you are in a group of more than 4 people or are travelling with kids it would be worth booking private Gran Canaria airport transfers. The normal taxis can only carry four people at a time and they very rarely have any kind of child seats. The private transfer company that we recommend are able to supply child safety seats on request.

Let us take the headache out of transportation. Your driver will greet you with your name on a sign board when you arrive, and provide friendly, reliable round trip private transfer to your destination. No waiting or luggage charges.

On outbound flights, your driver will meet you at your hotel or any other meeting point and transport you directly to the terminal.

Harbour

The beautiful Canary Island of Gran Canaria attracts tourism for numerous reasons, but one of the main attractions are the marinas in Gran Canaria.

Due to the seafaring nature of the people of the Canaries and the importance of the tourism sector, Gran Canaria has developed a very complete harbour infrastructure, which includes marinas and fishing havens.

Many of the latter also allow entry to leisure yachts, while all the harbours provide the basic services that make the prolonged mooring of vessels possible, in addition to the possibility of practicing the various water sports.

Las Palmas
Muelle Deportivo de Las Palmas
Tomás Quevedo Ramírez

35005 Las Palmas

Tel. 928 24 41 01

Fax. 928 24 36 06

Latitude 27º 7' N - Longitude 15º 25' W

Puerto de la Luz y Las Palmas, to give its official name, is a busy commercial port. The movement of all vessels is monitored from a control tower in the Port Authority building. If in any doubt one should contact Port Control on channel 16 or 10, who will then advise to switch to a working channel. Yachts entering or leaving should look out for commercial traffic, particularly the fast ferries.

The yacht harbour, Muelle Deportivo, lies at the southern end of the main harbour. It is administered by the Port Authority.

The yacht quay currently has 1.134 mooring places, which makes this the biggest yacht quay in the Canaries, and it is protected by two seawalls that give shelter to a surface area of 210.000 m2. The main seawall is 600 metres long and there are 70 stern-to-pier mooring places that can accommodate vessels with a maximum length of 45 metres. The enclosing seawall, which is also 600 metres long, has five floating quays with 150 mooring places that can each accommodate a maximum length of 16 metres. On the harbour side, which lies adjacent to the city, there are 12 floating quays, with a total of 864 mooring places for boats with a maximum length of 16 metres.

This quay, which is situated in the cosmopolitan and dynamic city of Las Palmas de Gran Canaria, within one of the most important commercial harbours in the Atlantic (although it is completely independent from the main harbour), is the ideal place for making preparations for Atlantic crossings, such as the ARC (Atlantic Rally for Cruisers) Regatta, which sets out from this harbour every year with 200 participants from different countries.

Entrance: the entrance into the marina is hard to detect and the situation is made more confusing by the entrance being marked by two red flashing lights, the one to be left to starboard being located at the eastern end of the northern breakwater, the other (port side) at the northern end of the main (southern) breakwater. Vessels should favour the starboard side of the narrow entrance as the port side is fouled and shallow.

Until the new reception dock becomes operational, arriving yachts should tie up at the Texaco fuel station at the northern end of the main dock where a port official will meet them and assign a berth. If arriving outside of office hours one should take one of the spaces on the main quay. One should not go to a pontoon unless instructed to do so by a port official.

Formalities are completed in the port office (Tel. 928 244 101) at the southern end of the marina. In 2006 the office will move to a new building at the entrance to the marina, next to the Texaco fuel station. The captain should report during office hours (0700 -1400 daily) with the ship's papers and passports. No other formalities are normally necessary for EU boats having only EU nationals on board. Crew members who are leaving the Canaries by air must take their passports to the immigration office (Policia de Frontera, Tel 928 264 431) located at the eastern end of the main Port Authority building (Edificio Autoridad Portuaria) in the port compound. This can be reached by taxi or bus no.1.

Docking

A reception dock will start being used in 2006. This will be located on the port side immediately past the marina entrance. The marina office is located here. The marina was refurbished in 2005 and a floating pontoon has been installed along the main quay making docking much easier. Larger yachts normally come stern-to the main quay after picking up a mooring buoy or dropping their own anchor. Yachts under 12 metres tie up to one of visitors' pontoons along the northern breakwater. There is water and electricity to all berths. There is a shower block, keys for which can be obtained from the port office. For stays longer than a month there is a discount, if port fees are paid in advance. It is also possible to anchor in the area north of the marina. Dinghies can be left at one of the pontoons.

Yacht Clubs

Club Maritimo Varadero de Gran Canaria

Joaquín Blanco Torrent - Muelle Deportivo

35005 - Las Palmas de Gran Canaria - Las Palmas

Tel. 928 24 99 19 / 928 24 99 20 - Fax. 928 23 12 65

Contact: Ms Maryluz Peñate. The club is situated in front of pontoon 12 which belongs to them. They ask 18€ per week to be a visiting member and use the club facilities

Arguineguín

Puerto de Arguineguín

35120 Arguineguín

Tel. 928 73 64 41

Fax. 928 73 64 41

Latitude: 27º 45' N - Longitude: 15º 41' W

The fishing harbour is used extensively by the cooperative Cofradia de Pescadores de Arguineguín and space for visiting boats is limited. The inner breakwater has been extended, but all spaces on the pontoons are taken up by local fishing boats. Visitors must anchor outside and take stern lines to the inner breakwater, or anchor in the well-protected area between the harbour and the beach.

Being located in one of the main tourist areas in the South of Gran Canaria, this harbour and the village in which it is situated have undergone considerable development, but without sacrificing the essential seafaring character of the village. The harbour is sheltered by a 429,33 metre-long seawall, which is used by the local fishing fleet as well as the boats that operate the regular sea routes. There are also 3 floating quays, which are used by the smaller fishing boats and pleasure boats.

The harbour provides 24-hour surveillance and all the mooring places have electricity and water supply. The dry dock has a 70-tonne travel lift, a crane with a capacity of 3 tonnes, workshops that do repairs and other businesses that supply ships.

Skippers are advised to enquire if there is space before they arrive, otherwise visiting yachts berth at the main wharf until a place is found for them. On arrival visitors must report to the port office, open 0800-1300, 1500-1700 Monday to Friday, Tel. 928 73 64 41, which is at the north end of the large shed on the dock, where the Cofradia also has its office. They will then be assigned a berth, yachts being usually accommodated at the main quay. There are a few moorings for yachts to come stern-to the outer breakwater which is fronted by large rocks.

Puerto Deportivo Taliarte

Puerto Deportivo Taliarte
35200 Telde
Tel. 928 21 93 00 / 928 37 21 44
Fax. 928 21 93 10

Longitude: 28º 00' N - Latitude: 15º 22,4' W

This fishing harbour, which falls under the jurisdiction of the Island Council of Gran Canaria, is located on the east coast, approximately 10 miles to the south of the city of Las Palmas de Gran Canaria and close to one of the main recreational areas of Telde, which includes the cosy beaches of El Hombre, Melenara and Salinetas. The harbour is sheltered by a 400 metre-long seawall with a ramp, which is used by the fishing fleet, while there are also 3 floating quays for small pleasure boats. The harbour provides 24-hour surveillance and the dry dock, which has a 25-tonne travel lift and a crane with a capacity of 1.5 tonnes, is run by the Cooperativa de Pescadores (Fishermen's Cooperative).

Puerto De Las Nieves

Puerto de Las Nieves
Edificio terminal, Agaete
Tel. 928 55 42 27
Fax. 928 55 42 27

Latitude 28º 06' N - Longitude 15º 43' W

Puerto de Las Nieves, which is located in the Northeast of the island, is the closest harbour to the island of Tenerife. It is for this reason that the harbour is currently being shared by the fishing fleet, pleasure boats and the high speed ferries that operate the regular routes between Gran Canaria and Tenerife.

The fishing village in which the harbour is situated is very popular among tourists and the local population alike, not only because of its charm, but also on account of the typical restaurants that line its streets and promenades.

The harbour provides 24-hour surveillance, while also having a ramp, a 70-tonne travel lift and a crane with a capacity of 1.5 tonnes.

The harbour is sheltered by a 616 metre-long seawall, which is shared by ferries and the bigger fishing boats, while the four 250 metre-long floating quays are for the smaller fishing boats and pleasure boats.

Puerto De Mogán

Puerto de Mogán
Torre de Control 1, 35138 Mogán
Tel. 928 56 56 68 / 928 56 51 51
Fax. 928 56 50 24
Latitude: 27º 49' N - Longitude: 15º 46' W

The harbour of Mogán is a modern yachting harbour that exists in perfect harmony with an apartment complex and a small hotel that are well known for their picturesque beauty.

The harbour's seawall is 275 metres long and provides shelter to a surface area of 36,560 m2. The harbour provides moorage to both leisure yachts and the local fishing fleet, for which an area is reserved at the rear of the marina. 36 of the 216 mooring places for leisure yachts are stern-to-pier and can accommodate boats with a maximum length of 45 metres, while a further 180 are distributed along 4 floating quays, accommodating boats with a maximum length of 20 metres. The harbour also has a large area for anchoring.

The harbour provides a 24-hour private surveillance service, as well as a postal service, public telephones, a laundry service, a supermarket, a medical service and meteorological information. There are also toilets and showers distributed throughout the marina. All the mooring places have water and electricity points, while there are also television connections on three of the four floating quays. There is a service station in the harbour and the dry dock has a 70 tonne travel lift, two 2.5 tonne cranes and a ramp.

The port monitors VHF channel 12 at all times, and uses channel 6 as a working channel. On arrival, visiting yachts should come alongside the reception dock on the starboard side of the entrance opposite the Mobil station and report to the marina office. This is located on the first floor of the three-storey control tower overlooking the reception dock Outside of office hours, there is a watchman patrolling the marina with a VHF radio tuned to channel 6. If directed to the outer mole, visitors should pick up a dead mooring and come stern to the floating dock.

Docking

Arriving boats should come alongside the reception dock on the starboard side as one enters the marina. Many of the moorings on the pontoons are privately owned, but the 190 metre long outer wharf is reserved for visitors. The marina has a capacity of just over 200 berths, of which 50% are available to visitors in summer and 20% in winter, the busier season. As Mogan is a popular port among transatlantic voyagers, those who wish to leave their boats here should reserve a place well in advance, especially during the busy season from the end of October to February.

All pontoon berths have water and electricity, also telephone connections and even a television and video link. There are showers and toilets on the outer quay reserved for visitors, for which a key must be obtained from the marina office. There are also showers and toilets on the ground floor of the control tower. A weather synopsis is posted every day on the notice board outside the marina office. Mogan operates its own inshore rescue service, the only such service on Gran Canaria's south coast, and has two large inflatable boats.

There is an anchorage east of the marina entrance which is occasionally used by cruising boats for short periods.

Opening Hours: 0800-1500 Monday-Friday, 0900-1300 Saturday

One of the most attractive marinas in the Canaries, Puerto Mogan is often full to capacity.

Puerto Deportivo De Puerto Rico

Puerto Deportivo de Puerto Rico
Puerto Rico Urbanization
35130 Puerto Rico
Tel. 928 56 11 41 / 928 56 16 32
Fax. 928 56 16 32
Latitude: 27º 47' N - Longitude: 15º 42' W

Puerto Rico is completely oriented towards the tourism sector. Everything has been designed with the aim of ensuring that a wide range of leisure and entertainment activities are within easy reach for the visitor, with a notable emphasis placed on water sports. This harbour consists of two piers that provide shelter to a surface area of 6 hectares. There are 531 mooring places that can accommodate boats with a maximum length of 60 metres.

The first pier has been designated as the Port-of-Call Pier and has a 100-metre long seawall that provides shelter to the beach and 212 mooring places. The first pier has three floating quays.

The new pier has been designated as the Base Harbour, having a 300-metre long seawall that provides shelter to 319 mooring places. The harbour has Blue Flag status and both piers have 24-hour surveillance. There is a service station and the harbour also provides a postal service, public telephones, a laundry service and meteorological information. All the mooring places have electricity, water and telephone connections (upon prior application), in addition to toilets and showers, which are distributed throughout the marina.

Leisure Activities. In this harbour, you can participate in a large variety of water sports. There are many motor and sailing boats that specialise in excursions to various parts of the coast. Puerto Rico is well known for its quiet sea and gentle winds, due to which this part of the coast is ideal for diving, parasailing and sailing. There are businesses where you can receive instruction in these sports or hire the equipment that is needed to practice them.

The waters of this area are also well known for its good deep-sea fishing conditions. In the harbour, you will find boats that are specially equipped for the enjoyment of this sport. In the bay, you can hire water skis for a jaunt around the bay, as well as jet skis, with which you can have some high-speed fun in a well-defined circuit.

Marina Anfi Del Mar
Marina Anfi del Mar
Barranco de la Verga

35120 Arguineguín

Tel. 928 15 07 98/928 15 29 90

Fax. 928 15 07 66/928 73 64 22

Latitude: 27º 46'16 N - Longitude: 15º 41'83 W

This marina, which is located in the Southwest of the island between Arguineguín and Puerto Rico, provides mooring for approximately 72 boats, and it is possible to rent a mooring place for the whole year.

The area in which the marina is located is one of the most enchanting parts of Gran Canaria, where looking at the yachts or renting a boat for a day or a weekend, or booking a place on an exclusive underwater fishing excursion can turn out to be an experience of a lifetime.
customerservice@anfi.es
Opening Hours: 08.30-20.00 daily

Club De Yates Pasito Blanco

Club de Yates Pasito Blanco

Crtra.C-812 Km.60, 35106 Maspalomas

Tel. 928 14 21 94

Fax. 928 14 25 46

Latitude = 27º 44'N - Longitude = 15º 37'W

Pasito Blanco marina lies to the south of the island's tourist beaches par excellence, which are delimited by the Maspalomas lighthouse.

The marina's seawall is 415 metres long, providing shelter to an area of 43,045 m2. There are a total of 387 mooring places, of which 102 are stern-to-pier, while a further 285 mooring places Club de Yates Pasito Blancoted along 6 floating quays. The stern-to-pier mooring places can accommodate boats with a maximum length of 40 metres, while the maximum boat length against the floating quays is 20 metres. The marina has been awarded Blue Flag status on account of the quality of its facilities.

The services that are provided by the marina include 24-hour surveillance, toilets and showers, a postal service, public telephones, a laundry service, weather forecast, electricity and water supply at all the mooring places and a petrol station. The dry dock is very large and well-equipped, and it has a 30 tonne travel lift and a 1.5-tonne crane.

Leisure Activities Pasito Blanco lies only a few kilometres away from the main tourist area of Gran Canaria and it is also the closest marina to the tourist area. There are businesses located within the marina that specialise in diving and motorboat excursions.

Water and electricity are laid to all berths and are included in the charges. There are hot water showers and toilets on the outer wharf and showers are also available in the boatyard. Long term rates being considerable lower than the daily rate and there is a 30% discount for stays over 6 months. The marina can provide a caretaker service for yachts laid-up afloat.

The marina is fairly isolated, which for some people is its main attraction. The gate into the resort is guarded 24 hours a day, making it a good place to leave a boat unattended for long periods.

The approaches and entrance to the marina are straightforward and Pasito Blanco Marina (Club de Yates de Pasito Blanco) keeps a 24-hour listening watch on VHF channel 6. On arrival, the skipper should report to the port office during office hours: 09.00-13.00 & 15.00-17.00 Monday to Friday, 09.00-13.00 Saturday

Ferries

On the southern part of Gran Canaria there are 2 ferries with regular service between >Arguineguin < > Puerto Rico < > Puerto de Mogan. A trip takes about 30 minutes.

Líneas Blue Bird

Ferry between Mogán - Puerto Rico - Arguineguín - Anfi

Marina Puerto Base
35130 Puerto Rico, Gran Canaria
Tel. 928 22 41 51 / 629 98 96 33 or 629 98 93 66

Líneas Salmon

Ferry between Mogán - Puerto Rico - Arguineguín

Marina Puerto Escala

35130 Puerto Rico, Gran Canaria

Tel. 649 91 93 83 or 649 92 59 18

Gastronomy

Gran Canaria is known worldwide for its excellent climate, its magnificent beaches and its astonishing landscape. However in the inland it keeps some treasures yet undiscovered for the visitor, and are related to their inhabitants, their culture and their way of life.

Among them, its gastronomy has been elaborated along several centuries with excellent raw materials (meat, fish, fruits and vegetables) and laid out in original and tasty recipes.

Thus, we invite you to make a trip trying some of the traditional dishes of Gran Canaria, starting by the "Enyesques" (snacks) among which we can find famous "Papas Arrugadas" (small potatoes boiled in their jackets), "Ropa Vieja" (type of casserole) or "Carajacas" (filleted liver). This can be followed by first courses such as "Fish Soup" or

"Watercress Soup". And the second courses can be composed of meat like "Salmorejo Rabbit", or fishes like "Sea Bream Casserole".

To end with we invite you sweeten your palate with any of the desserts like "Bienmesabe" (very sweet almond paste) or "Yolk Mass".

All this can go well accompanied with a good wine with O.D. "Gran Canaria" or "Monte Lentiscal".

With the recipes that we offer you here, you can try and cook some of these dishes at home, but really the best idea is to give yourself some holidays in Gran Canaria and enjoy our flavours in the restaurants that you will find in any spot of this island.

The traditional local cuisine is characterised for being a healthy and light diet. Goat meat, tollos en salsa, the ropa vieja or the delicious pork leg are served in any restaurant or "bar de tapas" (snack bar) for starters or snacks. But one of the most traditional dishes of the Canary cuisine is the "Sancocho Canario". The basic ingredients are the salty "cherne" (a type of fish), potatoes, sweet potatoes and "Gofio".

Local fruit and vegetables

The fruit and vegetables found in most shops, cafes and restaurants are grown locally using "normal" cultivation methods which often means that they have more flavour than visitors from Northern

Europe would normally expect.

When buying fruit and vegetables in the supermarket it is usually easy to tell the difference between the local and imported produce.

The imported stuff looks "perfect" - identical shape, identical colour, no marks or blemishes, and is often labelled "import".

The local produce comes in cardboard or wooden boxes, is delivered directly to the shops and markets by local farmers. The fruit is often misshapen. It usually tastes wonderful so don't turn your nose up, try it!

Bananas (Platanos)

The main local variety of banana is shorter and straighter than "the usual" banana, and are delicious.

Oranges (Naranja)

Choose the loose oranges which are not perfectly shaped. Ideal for making juice.

Avocados (Aguacates)

The avocados sold in Northern Europe are kept in cold storage for travelling and are ripened artificially.

The local avocados here come straight from the trees .. and you can really taste the difference.

Cactus fruit

The fruit of the local cactus is eaten in large quantities here, it is very juicy and contains many edible seeds. When you buy it in the shops the spines have usually been removed, otherwise lay them on the (sand) floor en brush them off with a stiff broom or hard brush. Keep it in the fridge for a few hours, then cut the ends off, slice the skin lengthways, peel the skin back and eat the centre.

Figs (Higos)

In the summer months fresh figs can be plucked directly from the trees - or bought in the shops. Don't eat the figs which hang in the sun, it may well give you 'tummy-trouble'. In the rest of the year dried figs can be bought either loose or plastic-wrapped.

Almonds (Almendras)

In the autumn, the almonds are harvested from the trees and kept in storage to be eaten throughout the year. They are often sold in small plastic bags in shops, or along the roadside. They are sometimes roasted, sometimes covered in salt or sugar.

Canaries make use of almonds in many things, desserts, biscuits, cakes, spreads, liquors etc. etc.

Tomatoes (Tomates)

When you taste the local tomatoes you will realise how much flavour is lost in the commercialisation of the growing process. If you grow your own tomatoes at home you will know what we mean.

Sweet Chestnuts (Castañe)

In season there is a good supply of sweet chestnuts which can be eaten fresh, or barbequed

Meat

Meat is for the Canaries an important part of the daily menu. They eat mainly pork, and also lamb, goat, rabbit and chicken. You will also find it on the menus of restaurants serving local food.

Goat (Cabrito)

Young goat is often served deep fried (Cabrito Frito) or in a stew (Cabrito en salsa).

Goat meat has a strong flavour, similar to lamb. It is usually eaten off-the-bone and the Canaries find it normal that you use your fingers.

Rabbit (Conejo)

Rabbit is often served in a stew/sauce, or in paella or fried.

Spreading sausage

You may see this soft spicy sausage in the meat display counters in long strings which are an almost orange colour. The spicy meat inside is squeezed out of its skin and spread on bread.

Sausage (Salchichó/Chorizo)

There is a wide variety of Spanish sausage available. Smaller quantities are available pre-packed in plastic, or from the meat counter, or you can buy a whole sausage and slice it yourself. It is mostly fairly hard and with a high fat content, and lots and lots of flavour.

Ham (Jamon)

There is the usual assortment of sliced ham, but you can get that at home so why not try the smoked ham ......

The Serrano is an Spanish speciality. It is often hung in meat shops and restaurants and sliced very very thinly. It can be a bit chewy but has an excellent taste.

Fish

Canary Islands are surrounded by the Atlantic ocean which provides a good variety of fish. Strangely the price is a bit high. Lots of different fish is available in tins.

Well-known and delicious to eat are the paella and the zarzuela. Some main fish are tuna, swordfish, sardines and octopus.

Cheese

On Gran Canaria the cheese is made from goats milk. There are very few cows on the island, largely due to the lack of pasture for grazing, so dairy products have to be imported. You can find all kinds of goat

cheese in the shops. Several of the islands have a typical cheese speciality of their own, best known are the smoked cheese of La Palma and Flor de Guía of Gran Canaria. **Potatoes, sauces and Gofio**
Potatoes grow well in Gran Canaria. Potatoes and yams, or sweet potatoes, are part of the staple diet. Farmers get 3 to 4 crops per year of the small potatoes varieties. They are often eaten with one or more sauces.

Potatoes are also used in the tortilla, the Spanish omelette. Another traditional "filler" is Gofio, a flour used in many ways.

Papas Arrugadas

Small, locally grown, potatoes cooked in their skins in water rich in sea salt. The salt residue can be seen on the crinkled skins. Usually eaten with mojo sauce.

Mojo verde

A sauce made of, among other things, green peppers, garlic and spices.

Mojo rojo

A sauce made of, among other things, red peppers, garlic and spices. There are soft and spicy versions.

You will notice differences in the taste of the mojos .... because each family has its own recipe.

Alioli

Garlic mayonnaise, also the taste of the Alioli is different in every restaurant.

Gofio

A kind of flour made from toasted and milled cereals. Used with milk for breakfast, in drinks, in meat dishes etc. Canaries say it is very healthy and many eat it every day!

Desserts

The most typical dessert is Bienmesabe, a mixture of honey, almond cream, eggs and rum. Besides that, you have a wide choice of tropical fruits, like papaya, avocado and mangoes. Platanos fritos (fried bananas) are also in great demand. Also, try the biscuits and meringues from Moya and the marzipan pralines from Tejeda.

Where to Eat

Gran Canaria is known worldwide for its excellent climate, its magnificent beaches and its astonishing landscape. However in the inland it keeps some treasures yet undiscovered for the visitor, and are related to their inhabitants, their culture and their way of life.

Among them, its gastronomy has been elaborated along several centuries with excellent raw materials (meat, fish, fruits and vegetables) and laid out in original and tasty recipes.

Thus, we invite you to make a trip trying some of the traditional dishes of Gran Canaria, starting by the "Enyesques" (snacks) among which we can find famous "Papas Arrugadas" (small potatoes boiled in their jackets), "Ropa Vieja" (type of casserole) or "Carajacas" (filleted liver). This can be followed by first courses such as "Fish Soup" or "Watercress Soup". And the second courses can be composed of meat like "Salmorejo Rabbit", or fishes like "Sea Bream Casserole".

To end with we invite you sweeten your palate with any of the desserts like "Bienmesabe" (very sweet almond paste) or "Yolk Mass".

All this can go well accompanied with a good wine with O.D. "Gran Canaria" or "Monte Lentiscal".

With the recipes that we offer you here, you can try and cook some of these dishes at home, but really the best idea is to give yourself some holidays in Gran Canaria and enjoy our flavours in the restaurants that you will find in any spot of this island.

The traditional local cuisine is characterised for being a healthy and light diet. Goat meat, tollos en salsa, the ropa vieja or the delicious pork leg are served in any restaurant or "bar de tapas" (snack bar) for starters or snacks. But one of the most traditional dishes of the Canary cuisine is the "Sancocho Canario". The basic ingredients are the salty "cherne" (a type of fish), potatoes, sweet potatoes and "Gofio".

Local fruit and vegetables

The fruit and vegetables found in most shops, cafes and restaurants are grown locally using "normal" cultivation methods which often means that they have more flavour than visitors from Northern Europe would normally expect.

When buying fruit and vegetables in the supermarket it is usually easy to tell the difference between the local and imported produce.

The imported stuff looks "perfect" - identical shape, identical colour, no marks or blemishes, and is often labelled "import".

The local produce comes in cardboard or wooden boxes, is delivered directly to the shops and markets by local farmers. The fruit is often misshapen. It usually tastes wonderful so don't turn your nose up, try it!

Bananas (Platanos)

The main local variety of banana is shorter and straighter than "the usual" banana, and are delicious.

Oranges (Naranja)

Choose the loose oranges which are not perfectly shaped. Ideal for making juice.

Avocados (Aguacates)

The avocados sold in Northern Europe are kept in cold storage for travelling and are ripened artificially.

The local avocados here come straight from the trees .. and you can really taste the difference.

Cactus fruit

The fruit of the local cactus is eaten in large quantities here, it is very juicy and contains many edible seeds. When you buy it in the shops the spines have usually been removed, otherwise lay them on the (sand) floor en brush them off with a stiff broom or hard brush. Keep it in the fridge for a few hours, then cut the ends off, slice the skin lengthways, peel the skin back and eat the centre.

Figs (Higos)

In the summer months fresh figs can be plucked directly from the trees - or bought in the shops. Don't eat the figs which hang in the sun, it may well give you 'tummy-trouble'. In the rest of the year dried figs can be bought either loose or plastic-wrapped.

Almonds (Almendras)

In the autumn, the almonds are harvested from the trees and kept in storage to be eaten throughout the year. They are often sold in small plastic bags in shops, or along the roadside. They are sometimes roasted, sometimes covered in salt or sugar.

Canaries make use of almonds in many things, desserts, biscuits, cakes, spreads, liquors etc. etc.

Tomatoes (Tomates)

When you taste the local tomatoes you will realise how much flavour is lost in the commercialisation of the growing process. If you grow your own tomatoes at home you will know what we mean.

Sweet Chestnuts (Castañe)

In season there is a good supply of sweet chestnuts which can be eaten fresh, or barbequed

Meat

Meat is for the Canaries an important part of the daily menu. They eat mainly pork, and also lamb, goat, rabbit and chicken. You will also find it on the menus of restaurants serving local food.

Goat (Cabrito)

Young goat is often served deep fried (Cabrito Frito) or in a stew (Cabrito en salsa).

Goat meat has a strong flavour, similar to lamb. It is usually eaten off-the-bone and the Canaries find it normal that you use your fingers.

Rabbit (Conejo)

Rabbit is often served in a stew/sauce, or in paella or fried.

Spreading sausage

You may see this soft spicy sausage in the meat display counters in long strings which are an almost orange colour. The spicy meat inside is squeezed out of its skin and spread on bread.

Sausage (Salchichó/Chorizo)

There is a wide variety of Spanish sausage available. Smaller quantities are available pre-packed in plastic, or from the meat counter, or you can buy a whole sausage and slice it yourself. It is mostly fairly hard and with a high fat content, and lots and lots of flavour.

Ham (Jamon)

There is the usual assortment of sliced ham, but you can get that at home so why not try the smoked ham ......

The Serrano is an Spanish speciality. It is often hung in meat shops and restaurants and sliced very very thinly. It can be a bit chewy but has an excellent taste.

Fish

Canary Islands are surrounded by the Atlantic ocean which provides a good variety of fish. Strangely the price is a bit high. Lots of different fish is available in tins.

Well-known and delicious to eat are the paella and the zarzuela. Some main fish are tuna, swordfish, sardines and octopus.

Cheese

On Gran Canaria the cheese is made from goats milk. There are very few cows on the island, largely due to the lack of pasture for grazing, so dairy products have to be imported. You can find all kinds of goat cheese in the shops. Several of the islands have a typical cheese speciality of their own, best known are the smoked cheese of La Palma and Flor de Guía of Gran Canaria.

Potatoes, sauces and Gofio

Potatoes grow well in Gran Canaria. Potatoes and yams, or sweet potatoes, are part of the staple diet. Farmers get 3 to 4 crops per year of the small potatoes varieties. They are often eaten with one or more sauces.

Potatoes are also used in the tortilla, the Spanish omelette.

Another traditional "filler" is Gofio, a flour used in many ways.

Papas Arrugadas

Small, locally grown, potatoes cooked in their skins in water rich in sea salt. The salt residue can be seen on the crinkled skins. Usually eaten with mojo sauce.

Mojo verde

A sauce made of, among other things, green peppers, garlic and spices.

Mojo rojo

A sauce made of, among other things, red peppers, garlic and spices. There are soft and spicy versions.

You will notice differences in the taste of the mojos .... because each family has its own recipe.

Alioli

Garlic mayonnaise, also the taste of the Alioli is different in every restaurant.

Gofio

A kind of flour made from toasted and milled cereals. Used with milk for breakfast, in drinks, in meat dishes etc. Canaries say it is very healthy and many eat it every day!

Desserts

The most typical dessert is Bienmesabe, a mixture of honey, almond cream, eggs and rum. Besides that, you have a wide choice of tropical fruits, like papaya, avocado and mangoes. Platanos fritos (fried bananas) are also in great demand. Also, try the biscuits and meringues from Moya and the marzipan pralines from Tejeda.

What to drink

Gran Canaria imports many products to drink, but don't miss out on the local produce.

Furthermore there are a few things that are worth knowing about what is "normal" here.

Water !!!

There are 2 water systems on the Island. "Main water" is supplied by local authorities and is used for the houses in towns and villages. "Natural water" is also used in country areas in the houses and on the land. Tourists are advised to buy bottled water.

And here's a very good tip: Cold water (drink) out of the fridge might seem refreshing and will cool you down, but it is important to realise, that it can have the opposite effect. Your body becomes cooler where the water reaches and its automatic reaction is to compensate for this by trying to warm your body up!

Natural water

There is a network of pipes, gullies and tanks on the island which brings the natural 'spring' water from the higher altitudes to farms, towns and villages on the lower parts of the island. The quality of the water is excellent, but the quality of pipes and tanks may not always be so good.

The tourist accommodations usually have good quality water. Tourists are usually advised to buy bottled water for drinking and making tea and coffee etc. The local water should be OK for cooking and bathing.

Tap water

The quality of the tap water varies from area to area. Water (in a few towns (areas)) can be drunk from the tap, but to be sure, check by the authorities. The quality of the water in the towns can vary from week to week. The usual chemicals are added.

Bottled water - still

Agua sin gas: There are several companies on the island that bottle the spring water and distribute it to shops, supermarkets, cafes and restaurants. It comes in plastic containers or glass bottles varying from 100 ml to 8 litres. Always take a bottle with you if you go walking or driving.

Bottled water - aerated

Agua con gas: This is the same as the "still water" but with bubbles added.

A very big part of the drinking water on this Island, originates in Aqua's de Firgas.

A company, which are doing much for the water is AquaLyng

The Water Supply on Gran Canaria

http://www.emalsa.es

The Management of the Water Supply on Gran Canaria

http://www.aguasgrancanaria.com

Wine

In the 16th century, the most famous of the wines that were exported from the Canary Islands were known as "malvasia" or simply "vino de Canarias" (wine from the Canaries). At present, a much more extensive range of wines are being produced on the island under the denomination of origin, "Monte Lentiscal", and the denomination of origin, "Gran Canaria". The grape varieties that are most widely cultivated are negra común, negramoll, tintilla, moscatel negra, malvasía and listan.

Both denominations encompass approximately twelve commercial brands that produce young, red and white wines. These magnificent wines have already conquered the local market and their fame is growing steadily.

One of the unique aspects of the island of Gran Canaria is the diversity of microclimates that are found on the island, which is why grapes of the same variety that are cultivated in a very small geographical area, present such a wide range of oenological characteristics. Another distinctive characteristic of the local wines is the fact that most of the vines were introduced onto the island before the occurrence of the phylloxera plague that devastated Europe's vineyards.

Consequently, it is possible to cultivate the vines without having to resort to grafting, which is why the island's viticulture enjoys certain unique characteristics.

The best way to get to know the wine culture of Gran Canaria is to visit the island's wine cellars. Some of these cellars have their own museums and virtually every cellar has tasting facilities, where you can buy the local wines directly. In many cellars, it is also possible for you to enjoy the local cuisine by prior reservation.

This "rebirth" of viticulture in Gran Canaria has been enriched by the inauguration of the Wine Museum, which is located in a house in the centre of Santa Brígida. This house is more than two centuries old.

Beer

There are no breweries on the island - the raw materials don't grow well here and anyway there is very little flat agricultural land.
The popular Spanish beers are Dorado, Tropical and San Miguel.
'Foreign beers' are widely available, with Heineken being the most popular.

Rum

The most popular drink in Gran Canaria is the rum, with or without cola (with cola, cuba libre); the town of Arucas holds the "Arehucas" factory; the Canarian had been producing the rum for hundred of years. It originates from the period that sugar cane was an important crop for the economy of the Canary Island, and they exported their "secret" of how to make it to South Americans during the colonization.

Ron Miel

A rum based honey liquor. Popular as an aperitif or a liquor after a meal. There are several manufacturers, and as with most things, the quality varies with the price. By the ones a little more expensive, available in the larger supermarkets.

Coffee

Coffee is popular on the island. Traditionally it is made with a percolator on the fire or stove, but that is time consuming so bars and cafes have machines for making it quickly. The beans are often fresh ground.

"Coffee break" in offices and shops is often taken in a local bar. This practice also encourages social contact.

Cafe solo

Strong black coffee served in small cups.

Cafe con leche

Coffee with warm milk served in larger cups. Note: This will almost certainly be pasteurised milk, as "fresh milk" is virtually unknown (See milk below).

Leche leche

Coffee with 2 types of milk; the pasteurised milk and a small amount of condensed milk. This usually does not need extra sugar.

Cortado

Almost as cafe con leche, but served in small glasses or tiny cups. Many Spaniards takes it as a little snack and empties the glass or the cup in one or two swallows.

Condensado

Coffee with condensed milk, is served in small glasses with a layer of condensed milk on the bottom and black coffee on top. Stir and wait before drinking. The stirring mixes the milk and coffee and the wait is to allow any coffee grains to settle to the bottom. This usually does not need extra sugar

Carajillo

Black coffee with local cognac. Usually served in small cups and can contain up to 50% spirits depending on your taste and the whim of the person who makes it.

Don't drink this if you are driving. The hot alcohol works fast.

Juices

Orange juice

Orange juice is normally made, while you wait, from local oranges. Served in a tall glass, with ice if you like it, a spoon for stirring and extra sugar in case you like it sweeter.

Milk

There are almost no dairy cattle on the island so don't expect "fresh milk", or bottled milk. It isn't part of the way of life here.

If you ask for fresh milk in a restaurant or bar you will probably get a strange reaction. It's about the equivalent of asking for goats milk in a northern European cafe ... they've probably heard of it, they never use it and nobody is daft enough to ask for it!

Pasteurised milk is available everywhere, and condensed milk is used for milk/sweetening in cooking, desserts and coffee.

Pasteurised milk

Widely available in supermarkets and shops and in a number of makes and types .. creamy, normal, half-fat, extra calcium and vitamins etc.

Condensed milk

Used in coffee and cooking, is available in shops and supermarkets and comes in many sizes including handy tubes.

Goats milk

Is widely used but seldom commercially available. You may be able to get some if you talk to the local people in the rural areas.

Goats cheese is widely available.

Wine

The Canaries do have their own wine too, even if is not very easy to believe. Lanzarote's wine is the most recognized, followed by the wine's from Tenerife, in la Orotava, they produced lots of it every year. Below the wine from Canary Island.

Gran Canaria

D.O. Monte Lentiscal & Gran Canaria

In the island of Gran Canaria there are wines of excellent quality, ideal for washing down any meal.

These wines have received two Spanish O.D. (origin denomination) certifications of their quality, which are "Monte Lentiscal" and "Gran Canaria".

On one side, the wines with O.D. "Monte Lentiscal" come from, as its own name indicates, the area of El Monte Lentiscal, in the inland zone and produce young, red and white wines, very fruity and with a strong bouquet. On the other side, wines with O.D. "Gran Canaria" are produced in different areas of the island excepting the zone of El Monte Lentiscal. This variety includes both red and white wines, being in general, young and fruity.

Visiting the Wine Cellars. The Wine Route

The best way to get to know the wine culture of Gran Canaria is to visit the island's wine cellars. Some of these cellars have their own museums and virtually every cellar has tasting facilities, where you can buy the local wines directly. In many cellars, you can also enjoy the local cuisine by prior reservation. This "rebirth" of viticulture in Gran Canaria has been enriched by the inauguration of the Wine Museum, which is located in a house in the centre of Santa Brígida that is more than two centuries old. (Visit the link below to Gran Canaria Wine)

Tenerife
D.O. Abona

This D.O. was officially recognized at the end of 1996. The district holds 2000 hectares vine fields, spread over a big area on the southern part of Tenerife, where the landscape is dry and rough.

The vineyards are situated in a height between 200 and 1600 meters, and are therefore placed among the highest in Europe.
The best and most well-balanced wines comes from the fields placed over 600 meters. Here the soil, being from volcanic origin, is fertile, dark and well-drained.

The sorts cultivated here are Listán Blanca (70%) and Listán Negra (30%).

D.O. Tacoronte-Acentejo
This D.O. is found in a perfectly bound area on the northern part of Tenerife. In the latest years it has gone through a heavy renovation, both regarding ways of production and structure of the companies.

The climate is affected by the Atlantic Ocean, moist but tempered. It is often raining, and there are many cloudy days, which together with the influence of the dew, gives more than sufficient water to the wine yards. The average temperature of the year is about 16 degrees, and there is a precipitation of 450 mm.

The wine yards lies on terraces on steep hills turning north towards the ocean, in a height at 200 - 800 meter. The soil, lying on volcanic underground, is reddish, very penetrating, rich in organic material and short of chalk.

The most important, recognised vines are the green Gual, Listán Blanco, Malvasía and Muscatel and the blue Listán Negro and Negramoll. The two blue grapes are preferred.

This D.O. produces following types of vine: white wine with 10 - 12,5% alcohol, traditionally macerated white-wine, carrying 12 - 14% alcohol, rosé-wines at 10,5 - 13% and red-wines at 12 - 14,5% alcohol. The most part of the wines in this D.O. are young, easy and fresh wines, but there also are wines stored by the general rules.

They are trying to export a little of these wines.

D.O. Valle De Güímar
This district, which by the way received D.O. Status in 1995, is situated on the south-eastern part of Tenerife. The vines grows in a big area, in a height of between 200 and 1600 meter. The best wines you get from the fields above 600 meter, where the earth and climate is best

situated to wine growing. The earth, being from volcanic origin, is fertile and well drained.

There is mostly made white wines, and the best of these are very interesting, with a good structure, soft taste and a fruity character.

So far wine hasn't been exported from this area.

D.O. Valle De La Orotava
This district lies on the northern part of Tenerife, in an exceptional beautiful area slanting from the lowest part of the Teide mountain towards the sea.

The vine is grown in a very original way, as the vine is plaited and makes up to 10 meter plaits. The earth, being from volcanic origin, is fertile and rich in basis and nitrogen, but poor in chalk, and it has a good ability to keep the moistness. The climate is generous, with sufficient rain.

The white wines, dominating in the western part of the district, are young wines, straw coloured with hints of amber in the colour and mild in the taste. The red wines, there are frequent in the eastern part, also are young, beautifully ruby in colour, easy, elegant and rich in fruits.

D.O. Ycoden-Daute-Isora

Inside this D.O. there are a handful of wine companies, able to produce some brilliant white wines. It is an active and technological well developed D.O.

This D.O. covers a big and characteristic area in the Northwestern part of Tenerife.

The volcanic earth, being fertile and of a fine physical nature affects the cultivated vines very much. This results in getting wines having a special bouquet.

Wine is grown from the coast to great heights, and the wine yards, placed the highest, enjoy special respect because of the fine quality of the wines, while wine growing in the lower regions are about to die out. About 1000 hectares are cultivated, and the method of growing vary after the place of the area.

The most important recognised drapes are the green Malvasía, Vijariego and Muscatel, and the blue Listán Negro, Negramoll and Malvasía Rosada.

There is produced white, rosé- and red wines with between 11%, 11,5% and 12% alcohol.

The area produces traditionally rosé wines, even if there to day also is produced white- and red wines. All the wines are young, with a fresh sourness and a fine balance in the taste. They distinguish by their big bouquet, having a distinctly flower like touch.

There are almost none export of these wines.

El Hierro
D.O. El Hierro
This D.O. is covering the whole of the Canary Island El Hierro, who has a tradition for wine-growing, documented all way back to the 17th Century. In the later years they use modern equipment and new methods of production, and thereby they have been able to overcome some weaknesses, which the wines from this area has had traditionally, and there is reached a level comparably to other canary districts. The D.O. status for the area was official recognised in 1996.

The vine grows on steep hills in the height of between 200 and 700 meter. Here the earth, being volcanic, loose and rather poor, but it has a relatively good ability to keep the moisture. The climate is temperate, rather dry in the lower areas and more moist higher up.

One produce white, red and rosé wine, one kind of each, and these wines are sold solely on the island.

La Palma
D.O. La Palma

D.O. La Palma covers 600 ha spread on the Island La Palma in a height of from 200 to 1000 meter.

The two most important sub-areas are the following:

Fuencaliente-Las Manchas, situated on the southern point of the Island and known for its Malvasías. Here the wine grows in ashes up the steep hills of the volcano.

The grades of grapes grown here, are Malvasía and Listán Blanco. From the Malvasísa is produced both sweet and dry wines with a outstandingly taste, and young white wines being very up to date.

Hoyo de Mazo-Las Breñas is situated on the eastern part of the Island. Here the cultivated earth is covered by volcanic rocks, as the vine are creeping over. You will get a very tasty redwine from the grape Negramoll.

Here is produced the so-called "vinos de tea" which trough the contact to the Canary pine during the production gets a touch of resin to the taste.

Wine from La Palma was never exported.

Lanzarote

D.O. Lanzarote

The typical wines from Lanzarote comes from wine-yards, cultivated under exceptional ecological conditions.

The production area includes 2000 ha. wine-yards and can be split in two sub areas: The central and southern part around La Geria, and the northern part Haría-Yé.

The wine-yards in the central and southern part is situated in an area covered by a thick, dark volcanic granulate (picón). In the bottom of some big pots, dug out in the earth, is planted 2 - 3 vines. More than the Picón protects the vines against the warm winds from Sahara, it is also, because of its ability to suck up moisture from the nights dew, able to give off water to the vines. This is essential to them in the very dry climate. The density of the vines is low, about 400 - 500 vines on each hectare.

The most important grape, cultivated here, is the legendary Malvasía, followed by the green grapes Diego and Listán Blanco, and the blue Listán Negro.

Together with the classical Malvasías, being stored, noble, amber or golden wines, and the sweet Malvasías or Moscateles, there are lately come fresh, young, perfumed white wines, having a big body and fineness, and which have great success. There's also a small production of rosé and redwine.

Wines have never been exported from this D.O.

Rules of storage for Spanish wines.
There are the following official storage names, as only the D.O. districts may use:

Crianza: Wine stored in casks and on bottles in at least 2 years, of this time at least 12 months in oak barrels.

Reserva: Red wine stored in cask and on bottles in at least 36 months, of this time at least 12 months in oak barrels. Regarding white- and rosé wines the periods are shorter.

Gran Reserva: Red wind stored in at least 24 months on oak barrels and furthermore at least 36 months on bottles. Also here the periods are shorter for rosé- and white wines.

In some of the D.O. districts there are longer storage periods than here mentioned.

Small Spanish List of words

Vino de mesa = table wine

Vino fino de Mesa = better table wine

Vino corriente or Vino commùn or Vino de pasto = normal table wine, the French's wine ordinaries

Vino de marka = Named wine, bottled in a bodega, having a certain responsibility and name.

Vino rancio = strong, older "sour" wine

Vino de agujas = a little sparkling

Vino verde = a little sparkling wine (in Portugal it is called *Vinho verde* with an h)

Vino generoso = is a stronger wine with 18 - 20 % alcohol or more.

Vino tinto = red wine

Vino tintillo = pink wine

Claret = also a pink wine

Rosado = rosé

Blanco = white

Espumoso = sparkling

Abocado and Dulce = both means sweet

Seco and bruto = both means dry

Restaurant & Bar

Nightlife

The nightlife of Gran Canarias is a busy affair and it caters well to its tourist population with plenty of bars and nightclubs as well as a huge selection of restaurants to choose from.

The nightlife here is typical of any party island - noisy, lively and lots and lots of fun. It starts late and goes on all night. Most bars stay open till 02.00am and the discos stay open till at least 06.00am or more. Things normally kick off around midnight. It's fairly quite up to this point, so don't start drinking too early or you'll be in a terrible state!!

It's impossible to get bored here. Head off to Playa del Ingles and Maspalomas and you'll see hundreds of bars, clubs and discos for all different tastes.

The vast array of bars, clubs and restaurants in the biggest beach resort, Playa del Ingles, is a major attraction for the young and lively crowd, and also the resort of Puerto Rico has lots of British pubs and cafes, as well as a variety of English clubs.

A night out in Gran Canaria is not especially expensive, beer prices are cheap and spirit portions are generous, while wine by the bottle is a very affordable way to get a little merry.

Most of the action is happening in and around the big shopping centres. The variety is enormous. You'll be spoilt for choice. If you don't like one, move on to the other. There are free entrance fliers everywhere! As you approach the main nightlife areas people (usually pretty girls) will come up to you and give you flyers offering concessions into their bar, disco or nightclub. Normally the first drink is free.

Playa del Ingles has a lively gay scene. Check out the Yumbo Centre; it's one of the most popular and well-known gay areas on the island. They play some great tunes here too. The Kasbah Centre is more for young people and the Plaza Shopping Centre is where you go to hear the latest international music.

Las Palmas is also buzzing at night, but it's a long way from the main beach holiday resorts in the south of Gran Canaria. If you are staying in Las Palmas, there are a number of places that are well worth checking out, Plaza de España, in particular. It's located in the Mesa y Lopez district. It's a very lively square and stays busy well into the early hours.

In Las Palmas, there's the Casino Las Palmas in Hotel Santa Catalina. In San Agustin, there's the Gran Canaria Casino, which you'll find in Hotel Meliá Tamarindos.

Bars & Pubs

Gran Canaria is a very cultural place with a very diverse range of people and visitors within its borders. Gran Canaria is unique in that it caters for everyone no matter what the taste is.

The popular tourist areas are home to a large selection of restaurants, with some high class establishments located in Las Palmas. Expensive doesn't necessarily mean delicious or authentic however, and if you really want a true a taste of traditional cuisine, you will need to seek out the smaller establishments where the locals hang out. Restaurants don't get busy of an evening until about 21.00 and it's not unusual for diners to still be eating around 23.00.

Vast range of foods
Restaurants in Gran Canaria offer a vast range of foods from across the globe from Indian, Chinese, Thai, American, traditional English and European, Japanese, and Mexican as well as Fast food, fine dining and much much more.

The variety and quality of places to eat are second to none on the Canary Islands. With a diversity of food to satisfy the hungriest appetite, or the most discerning palates, from the humble Fish and Chips to a gourmet banquet prepared by top chefs from around the world.

You will also find that most restaurants have excellent wines, including the locally produced, as well as a selection of beers and spirits.

Caught fresh every day, fish is a speciality on the Canary Islands having always been one of the staples of these seafaring people. Why not treat yourself to one of the many fish dishes cooked in the traditional Canarian style, usually served with a Mojo sauce, either hot and spicy or garlic, this is accompanied by fresh local vegetables and fruit, a pleasure not to be missed during your stay.

For instance during your holiday in the Canary Islands, why not try a Tapas, an ideal quick snack or light meal with a difference, consisting of small portions of main meals such as meat balls, fried squid or cured ham. The best way to try them is to choose two or three different ones, a good idea if there is a group of you, that way you will have maybe a dozen different dishes to share. A great way to sample the local food.

With a culture as diverse as Gran Canarias, you will never be stuck for something new or different to try, and that is why Gran Canaria is such a great place to eat out.

Restaurants

Gran Canaria is a very cultural place with a very diverse range of people and visitors within its borders. Gran Canaria is unique in that it caters for everyone no matter what the taste is.

The popular tourist areas are home to a large selection of restaurants, with some high class establishments located in Las Palmas. Expensive doesn't necessarily mean delicious or authentic however, and if you really want a true a taste of traditional cuisine, you will need to seek out the smaller establishments where the locals hang out. Restaurants don't get busy of an evening until about 21.00 and it's not unusual for diners to still be eating around 23.00.

Vast range of foods
Restaurants in Gran Canaria offer a vast range of foods from across the globe from Indian, Chinese, Thai, American, traditional English and European, Japanese, and Mexican as well as Fast food, fine dining and much much more.

The variety and quality of places to eat are second to none on the Canary Islands. With a diversity of food to satisfy the hungriest appetite, or the most discerning palates, from the humble Fish and Chips to a gourmet banquet prepared by top chefs from around the world.

You will also find that most restaurants have excellent wines, including the locally produced, as well as a selection of beers and spirits.

Caught fresh every day, fish is a speciality on the Canary Islands having always been one of the staples of these seafaring people. Why not treat yourself to one of the many fish dishes cooked in the traditional Canarian style, usually served with a Mojo sauce, either hot and spicy or garlic, this is accompanied by fresh local vegetables and fruit, a pleasure not to be missed during your stay.

For instance during your holiday in the Canary Islands, why not try a Tapas, an ideal quick snack or light meal with a difference, consisting of small portions of main meals such as meat balls, fried squid or cured ham. The best way to try them is to choose two or three different ones, a good idea if there is a group of you, that way you will have maybe a dozen different dishes to share. A great way to sample the local food.

With a culture as diverse as Gran Canarias, you will never be stuck for something new or different to try, and that is why Gran Canaria is such a great place to eat out.

Nature

Beaches

Gran Canaria - 60 Kilometres of the Most Beautiful Sandy Beaches

If you are looking for a relaxing beach holiday or to visit the beach during you active holiday then look no further. The love for Gran Canaria has reasons: Almost 60 of the 236 kilometres of Gran Canaria's coastline consist of beaches of various descriptions, ranging from the impressive Maspalomas beach, where you can find 250 hectares of sand dunes right next to the sea, to the concealed and unspoilt beach of Güi Güi, as well as the lively beach in the capital, namely the Las Canteras beach.

As a result of the temperate climate and agreeable temperatures of the bathing waters (ranging between 18ºC during winter months and 22ºC during the rest of the year) it is possible to enjoy the beaches throughout the year.

The beaches of the Island are mentioned below, with information about Naturist beaches and with a blue flag

Once you arrive and before you burn your skin, use a skin protection crème. Start with at least factor 15, or more is better (30 is not to much). To expose unprotected skin on direct sunlight could be very dangerous. Children under 4 years must stay in shadow. Protect yourself and than relax on the beach.

When bathing you have to be very careful, and respect the placed flags, as there can be a very strong underwater current.

Red flag:	Bathing prohibited

Gran Canaria Environment

Yellow flag:	Bathing on your own responsibility - Be very careful
Green flag:	Bathing ok. - Good conditions
No flag:	Bathing on your own responsibility - Be very careful

Gran Canaria list of Beaches around the island

	Length	Breadth	Degree of coverage	Area
Agaete				
Playa del Juncal	120	25	Medium	Rocky
Playa Turman	20	5	Medium	Rocky
Playa Las Salinas	90	5	Medium	Rocky
Playa Las Nieves I	250	29	High	Harbour
Playa Las Nieves II	210	45	High	Rocky
Playa de Guayedra	200	48	High	Rocky
Playa de Sotavento	200	34	Low	Rocky
Playa Farenoque	240	30	High	
Playa del Risco	415	41	Medium	Rocky
Playa Segura				

Playa del Muelle				
Playa de la Caleta				
Agüimes				
Playa Arinaga	700	70	High	City
Playa El Cabrón	290	27	Medium	Rocky
Playa Balos	1000	12	Low	Rocky
Playa Vargas	1300	15	Low	Rocky
Arguineguín				
Playa de Arguineguín	100	25	High	City
Playa Patalavaca	290	25	High	City
Playa Aquamarina	85	23	High	City
Playa La Verga	120	20	High	City
Playa Las Marañuelas	360	14	High	City
Artenara				
Playa Punta Gongora	440	20	Medium	Rocky
Playa Punta Arena	1200			

Gran Canaria Environment

Arucas				
Playa San Andres	450	10	Low	
Playa Los Enanos	310	10	Medium	
Playa El Peñon	150	5	Medium	Rocky
Playa Quintanilla	300	13	Medium	Rocky
Playa Los Marrajos	130	20	Low	
Playa La Fuente	170	50	Low	
Playa Las Coloradas	80	3	Low	Rocky
Playa Los Charcones	110	10	High	Rocky
Playa El Puertillo	360	20	High	
Playa Charco Las Palomas	60	10	Low	
Playa Las Salinas	210	30	Medium	
Gáldar				
Playa Juncal	120	25	Medium	Rocky
Playa Punta Gorda	50	15	Low	
Playa La Guancha	25	3	Low	
Playa Lagarto	200	20	Low	

Playa Risco Partido	30	4	Low	Rocky
Playa Martorell	80	140	Low	
Playa Sardina	80	40	High	
Playa El Muelle	80	9	Low	Rocky
Playa El Roquete	60	15	Low	Rocky
Playa Paso del Salgo	15	3	Low	
Playa Punta del Faro	85	20	Low	
Playa Caleton de los Cangrejos	50	25	Low	
Playa Punta Galdar	85	15	High	
Playa Caleta de Abajo	130	25	Medium	
Playa Punta del Clavo	75	25	Medium	Rocky
Playa Furnia	70	40	Medium	
Playa Dos Roques	140	30	Medium	Rocky
Playa Boca Barranco	255	40	Medium	Rocky
Playa El Agujero	230	50	Medium	Rocky
Playa La Redonda	45	30	Low	
Playa La Caleta de Arriba	40	30	Medium	

Ingenio

Gran Canaria Environment

Playa El Burrero	500	40	Medium	
Playa de Las Torrecillas				
La Aldea de San Nicolás				
Playa Los Secos	260	25	Low	
Playa Ambar	220	17	Low	
Playa Tasarte	710	23	High	Rocky
Playa Aneas	60	15	Low	
Playa Tasartico	465	20	High	Rocky
Playa Descojonado	50	8	Low	
Playa Lioguicha	240	15	Low	
Playa Güi-Güi Chico	350	25	Medium	
Playa Güi-Güi Grande	360	25	Medium	
Playa La Aldea	720	25	High	
Playa Puerto La Aldea	30	5	High	
Las Palmas				
Playa Boca Barranco	260	10	High	Rocky
Playa Las Canteras	2250	50	High	

Playa El Confital	180	25	Low	Rocky
Playa Alcaravaneras	550	85	High	
Playa San Cristobal	950	28	Low	
Playa La Laja	1200	40	High	Rocky
Playa Los Muellitos	70	40	Medium	
Playa La Cicer	520	50	Medium	
Maspalomas				
Playa Maspalomas	2710	75	High	
Playa El Faro	560	20	High	
Playa Las Mujeres	500	30	High	
Playa Las Meloneras	460	75	High	Rocky
Playa Pasito Blanco	450	40	High	
Mogán				
Playa Costa Alegre	90	30	High	
Playa La Carrera	40	22	High	
Playa Medio Almud	50	8	High	Rocky
Playa Tiritaña	80	12	High	Rocky

Gran Canaria Environment

Playa Cruz de Piedra	60	24	Medium	Rocky
Playa Taurito	190	53	High	
Moya				
Playa Charco San Lorenzo	75	45	High	Rocky
Playa San Lorenzo	920	35	High	Rocky
Playa Caleta de Moya	240			
Playa del Ingles				
Playa del Ingles	2700	50	High	
Puerto de Mogán				
Playa Mogan	190	35	High	
Playa Veneguera	370	40	High	Rocky
Playa Los Secos	260	25	High	
Puerto Rico				
Playa Balito	150	14	Medium	
Playa Puerto Rico	250	90	High	

Playa Amadores	185	29	High	
Playa Tauro	440	30	High	Rocky
Playa El Cura	225	38	High	
San Agustin				
Playa San Agustin	670	70	High	
Playa Tarajalillo	2240	30	Medium	
Playa El Aguila	430	40	High	
Playa El Besudo	170	35	High	
Playa Las Burras	300	110	High	
Playa Bahía Feliz	60			
San Bartolomé de Tirajana				
Playa Boca Las Casillas	1700	20	Low	
Playa Corral de Espino	1450	20	Low	
Playa El Cardon	1500	27	Low	
Playa El Cochino	250	20	High	
Playa Montaña de Arena	250	38	High	
Playa Las Carpinteras	160	24	Medium	Rocky

Playa Triana	490	20	High	Rocky
Playa Los Bigotes	75	21	Medium	
Playa Llanillo	280	20	Medium	
Playa El Lomo Galeon	50	18	Medium	
Playa El Molinero	180	18	Medium	
Playa Santa Agueda	240	24	Medium	
Playa Ganaguin	90	25	High	
Playa El Pirata	400			
Playa La Caleta	100			
Playa Llano de los Militares	250			Rocky
Playa Pasito Bea	85			Rocky
Santa Lucía de Tirajana				
Playa El Arenal - Pozo Izquierdo	1280	20	Low	
Santa María de Guía				
Playa La Caleta de Arriba	40	30	Medium	
Playa Roque Prieto	40	10	High	Rocky
Playa Punta del Angosto	175	20	Low	

Playa San Felipe	450	25	High	Rocky
Playa Pagador	310	36	High	Rocky
Playa El Roque	410	7	Medium	
Playa El Altillo	120	21	High	Rocky
Playa Boquini	480	15	Low	Rocky
Telde				
Playa Jinamar	975	50	High	
Playa El Barranquillo	550	48	Low	
Playa San Borondon	225	30	Low	
Playa Chica	120	36	Low	
Playa La Garita	260	25	High	
Playa Pozuelo	130	45	High	
Playa El Hombre	270	65	High	
Playa Melenara	350	50	High	
Playa Salinetas	320	50	High	
Playa Agua Dulce	140	20	Low	Rocky
Playa Tufia	110	20	Medium	
Playa Ojos de Garza	450	45	Medium	

		82		

Fauna

Gran Canaria possesses many natural resources in addition to its beaches, which is why this is the perfect place for getting in touch with nature, there being a wide variety of possibilities and activities in which one can participate. Gran Canaria, (although small only 1,532 square kilometres) has a widely varying

topography, climate, flora and fauna. There are species of animals indigenous to the archipelago, along with a rich tapestry of history.

Almost 43% of the territory of Gran Canaria is protected. This means approximately 66,571 hectares of land, which is almost 1,000 square metres of protected land for each inhabitant of the island. Due to the geological formation of the interior of the island, the landscapes of the interior are very different from those of the coast, originating many and varied ecosystems on the island.

An anecdotal piece of information is that only 1% of the island's population lives on protected land. The Parque Rural del Nublo is an interesting case in this regard. This rural park, which stretches over eight municipal areas in the centre of the island and covers a surface area of 26,307.4 hectares (the size of La Gomera island), but it supports a tiny population of around 5,000 inhabitants. This fact is ironic in the light of the environmental problems caused by overpopulation on Gran Canaria, mainly in the Northeast of the island where the greatest part of the population lives.

Topography

The volcanoes that form the islands' backbone saw the light of day at about the time the Atlas Mountains were formed in North Africa millions of years ago. The highest volcano, Teide at 3718 m on Tenerife, is Spain's tallest peak and the third tallest volcano in the world after two in Hawaii. All the volcanic activity has ensured that the soil is very fertile, but there are no rivers and the islands have been periodically plagued by water shortages. Most of the drinking water on some islands comes straight from desalination plants.

Being of volcanic origin, the island's orography has a conical shape that is split in two by the ravines of Tirajana and Agaete, representing the main line of division that separates the enormous contrasts of the North and the South. Numerous ravines gouge their way across the centre of the island in the direction of descent.

This feature, together with the complicated relief and the massif (known as Los Pechos) that runs from the north-west to the south-west, are the main architects of the great variety of climatic conditions that exist on this island and, therefore, the great variety of ecosystems to which the island is host.

Tourism

The inhabitants of the islands have put together a supply of nature tourism that is characterised by an equally deep respect for the environment. This includes everything from century-old country houses that have been renovated, as well as a wide range of leisure activities that include everything from high risk sports, such as rock climbing, to hiking along the "Caminos reales" or ancient network of country pathways, which has been reopened for use by the public and which forms part of the cultural and historic heritage of the island.

Climate

The Canaries bask in an eternal-spring climate, with temperatures ranging from 18°C (64°F) in winter to 24°C (75°F) in summer. On a hot day at the beach, it can still be pleasantly cool if you get up into the mountains, and you'll definitely need warm clothes if you reach any high altitudes during the winter

Except for Lanzarote and Fuerteventura, the northern side of the islands is sub-tropical, while the south, including the first two mentioned islands, is drier and slightly warmer. There is not much rain except on parts of the windswept northern coasts, and what there is tends to fall on the northern side of the more mountainous islands.

The flat islands, with no mountains to trap rain clouds, hardly receive a drop of rain. On occasion, especially in summer, the sirocco (the hot wind from the Sahara) blows in from Africa, turning day into twilight and coating everything with grime. It's at its worst in the eastern islands, and is known locally as the calima.

In Gran Canaria one can do anything, from hiking through the most beautiful nature areas to taking part in adventure sports, or merely contemplating the hundreds of indigenous species that are unique in the world. In Gran Canaria, anything is possible for those who want to satisfy their need to get in touch with Mother Nature.

The following are some of the nature areas on Gran Canaria that deserve special mention:

Natural Areas

Monumento Natural de Bandama (Natural Monument):
This nature area, which covers a surface area of 325.7 hectares,

includes parts of the municipal areas of Las Palmas de Gran Canaria (the capital), Santa Brígida and Telde

Parque Rural del Nublo (Rural Park):
This is the largest protected nature area on the island. The 26,307.4 hectares of this park are spread over eight municipalities, namely Tejeda, La Aldea de San Nicolás, Mogán, San Bartolomé de Tirajana, Artenara, San Mateo, Valleseco and Moya

Parque Natural de Tamadaba (Nature Park):
This nature park, which covers a surface area of 7,538.6 hectares, with its pine groves, lies within the municipalities of Agaete and La Aldea de San Nicolás.

Parque Rural de Doramas (Rural Park):
Covers an area of 3,586 hectares in the municipal areas of Moya, Valleseco, Firgas, Santa María de Guía, Arucas and Teror
The long catalogue of protected areas on Gran Canaria is completed by the Natural rural monuments of Montañón Negro, Roque Aguayro, Tauro and Arinaga.

There are also a number of areas that have been declared as "Natural Rural Landscapes", namely La Isleta, Pino Santo, Tafira, Las Cumbres, Lomo Magullo, Fataga and Montaña de Agüimes.

Lastly, there are a number of areas that have been declared as "Areas of Interest", these being Jinámar, Tufia, Roque de Gando and Juncalillo del Sur.

Terrestrial fauna

Reptiles

The terrestrial fauna of the Island is characterised by the absence of big vertebrates and harmful species. Birds and reptiles are the most numerous species of Gran Canaria wildlife. Among the vertebrates we have the Canary Island lizard - endemic of the island and whose abundance is overwhelming, the Gran Canaria skink, Boettger's Canary wall gecko and Osorio shrew.

Birds

Birds have the biggest representation in the Island's wildlife population: specifically, 48 species including the nesting birds of this island, with endemic birds such as great spotted woodpeckers, robins and the blue chaffinch, the latter in the pine forests of Pilancones-Inagua.

The canary bird deserves a separate mention due to its symbolic establishment that relates it both to the Canary Islands and to Gran Canaria in particular. The interesting thing about this bird, with a great singing ability, is that it was bred through crossbreeding with other species, thus producing a great variety.

Besides, the Island is a resting place for many of the migrating birds.

We can point out the birds included in the marine and nesting species.

Marine fauna

The marine fauna of Gran Canaria is very rich and diversified in species, and this peculiarity is a result of the environmental diversity and the geographical situation of the island.

One of the distinct features of the marine settlements of the waters of Gran Canaria is the coexistence of species such as pelagic fish and turtles.

The Caretta species is conspicuously the most common of the family turtles. These species coexist with rays, manta rays, stingrays and angel sharks, swordfishes, big tuna fish or coastal species such as white sea breams, parrot -fishes, goldlines, saddled sea breams, pompanoes, groupers, blacktail combers, john dories or pollacks.

Within the mammals that are found in the waters of Gran Canaria are common dolphins, bottlenose dolphins and whales.

Flora

The Flora of the Canary Islands is unique because of its diversity. There are about 1900 kinds of plants on the Islands of which about 800 are represented on Gran Canaria.

Here is a view covering the different plants, listed below:

Agave - Aloe - Avocado tree - Bamboos - Banana - Barilla - Bougainvillea - Dragon blood tree - Eucalyptus - Fig cactus - Flamboyant - Hibiscus - Poinsettia - Coffee - Canarian Harebell - Canarian Palm - Canarian Scotch Pine - Potatoes - Laurel - Heather - Onion - Almond Tree - Mango tree - Mulberry tree -
Oleander - Orchilla - Papaya - Thorn Apple - Senecio - Sugar Cane - Column-Euphorbia - Tamarisk - Tomato

Agave (Aga`vaceae) The name originates from the Greek agavos = admirable, excellent, and is referring to flowering plants. Agaves can be found everywhere in the dry parts of the Islands. It will take from 10 - 20 years before, from the strong, fleshy leaves, long flower stems are going high, often more than 10 meter up. When the flowering is over, the plant will die, but will shoot much in its lifetime.

Aloe (Lili'aceae) The Greek Aloe means bitter, and refers to the leaves juice, which has been used as medicine, spice and skin lotion. Aloe Vera can be separated into two basic products: gel and latex. Aloe

Vera gel is the leaf pulp or mucilage, a thin clear jelly-like substance obtained from the parenchymal tissue that makes up the inner portion of the leaves. The gel contains carbohydrate polymers, plus various other organic and inorganic compounds. Aloe gel has been used for topical treatment of wounds, minor burns, and skin irritations. American consumers are most familiar with aloe's use in skin-care products. Aloe products for internal use have been promoted for everything from , headaches, to arthritis, and many other conditions.

Avocado tree (Lau'raceae) or Aguacate, which is the Spanish name, originates from Tropical America, but is able to grow in subtropical areas, and therefore also on the Canary Islands.
On the Islands the green colour of the avocado pears are common in the household.
They are used in different salads and are also eaten as a starter with salt and pepper.

Bamboo (Gra´mineae) the highest grass in the world, with hollow, three like stalks, are growing in low places on the islands, where there are sufficient water, often in connexion with the watering plant in the banana plantations. The stalks, which in the tropical areas becomes 15 - 20 meter high, will in the Canary Islands become about 2 - 3 meter high.

Banana (Mu´saceae). The botanical name for banana is Musa, and the growing of bananas on the Islands is an important industry. It is said, that the plant was brought here from Guinea in the 1500 Hundreds, where it was used as an normal plant in the gardens, but as more hardy kinds was developed, it was in the end of the 1800 Hundreds one of the most important export articles on the Island.

Bananas from the Canary Island are smaller and more sweet than the bananas we normally buys in the shops, and as a whole it is the plant we mostly are connecting with the Canaries. In Spanish the plant is called Platano. With its stem and the broad leaves, it mostly reminds you of a tree, but it really is a "herbaceous perennial", where the stem actually is formed of the leaf sheaths, which together with the leaves die down when the fruit is ripe.

12 - 14 months after the plant is planted, the first and only inflorescence is produced. A bunch of bananas is ripe ion about 6 months, and every plant gives only one bunch of bananas. The old plant dies, but before that it has developed a sucker, that can be used in the propagation.

Barilla (Aizo´acae) is a so called purple plant, where the flowers come out in the middle of the Day, or when the sun is very strong.

Mesembryanthemum nodiflorum and Mesembryanthemum crystallinum are growing in the lowest part of the drought plants zone on barren soil. There are more kinds of the plant, also in the Canary Islands called cofe-cofe, cosco and vidrio. In earlier times, when there were a draught and it was difficult to get food, one roasted the seeds of the Barilla, and produced a special Gofio, which was used as a surrogate of the normal Gofio, produced from corn. To day the plant is looked upon as a weed.

Bougainvillea (Nyctagi'naceae) is originally an Brazilian liana, whose flowers are placed 3 and 3 together. Every flower is placed on the middle string of a coloured high leave, and this beautiful climbing plant are planted of most Canaries and newcomers as red, purple, orange or white flowers.

Dragon blood tree (Aga´vaceae) Dracaena Draco is the most remarkable tree you can find on the Canary Islands. The sap of the tree is blood-red and was in ancient times used to embalm the dead or to produce medicine.

The tree has an strong trunk and the leaves are fleshy and pointed like a spear. For the Islands indigenous population the dragon blood tree was sacred. There are only a few left, among other places at Icod de los Vinos on Tenerife and in Gáldar on Gran Canaria. The one in Gáldar is said to have been planted in 1718, and therefore it is the oldest tree on Gran Canaria.

Eucalyptus (Myr'taceae) Eucalyptus globulus comes from Australia. It was called the Fever tree, because it could keep the Malaria-fever at bay. It is planted in swamped areas, suck the water and helps to dry out the swamps and thereby drive the mosquitoes away. It is able to turn its silver shining leaves, so they catch the sunrays the least. The cones will be found on the ground and smell delicious. (Take a few in your pocket, and you will always have something nice to smell. Among other it is used in eucalyptus pastilles and in ointments against rheumatism.

Fig cactus (Cac'taceae) Opuntia ficus india is a cactus from Mexico, which was introduced on the Canary Islands in the 16. century. Fig cactus can be 3 - 4 meter high. The fruit is in Spanish called chumbo, and the plant chumbera. The Fig cactus was originally imported as a host for the small scale insect cochenillen. This small parasite (cactus cacty) is used by colour factories to produce a red colour.

On the Canary Island it is used as a very effective quickset hedge.

The Fig cactus produce yellowish flowers, that turns to edible fruits. A ripe fig cactus is succulent and sweet. You should always use glows, when you clean the fruits, and very carefully take all the needles and eyes on the surface away. The very fine thorn goes through the skin and is hold in place by barbs. The fruit is used in salads, to desserts and is used in marmalade

Flamboyant (Papilio'naceae) Delonix'regia is a fast growing, smallish tree with a very broad crown. The tree is easily recognised by the scarlet flowers and the shiny brown pea shells, which can reach a length at 50 cm. and a width at 5-6 cm. Even when it is a tropical tree, which normally belongs in the rain forest on Madagascar, it is doing fine in dry areas, without rain in several months.

Hibiscus (Mal'vaceae) Hibiscus rosa-sinensis is in the same family as hollyhock originates from the East Indies. It has big colourful flowers and is used much in tropical and subtropical areas as an ornamental bush, in hedges and as small trees in gardens and parks. There are different kinds whose flowers are both single and double. The colour of the flowers varies from red, yellow, Rosa, white and spotted.

Poinsettia (Euphorbi'aceae) Euphorbia pulcherrima originates in Mexico but is cultivated as an ornamental bush everywhere in tropical and subtropical areas. In the Canary Islands the plant can grow to several meters in height, and is a ornamental plant in many gardens and parks. The flowers are small and is hardly noticeable, but in turn you notice the scarlet leaves, named braktees. There are different kinds with white and pink braktees.

Driving through Mogan you will see some trees with double flowers.

Coffee (Rubi'aceae) Coffee Arabica is a deciduous tree, which can reach 10 meters in height. There is only grown a little coffee in the Canaries, but the plant is to be found some places, (also as a tree) It has got white flowers and red fruits as big as cherries.

The coffee beans is the two fruits which is in every fruit. Canary coffee is bitter to the taste.

Canarian Harebell (Campanu´laceae) is a bush with big scarlet flowers, flowering from January to April.

Canarian Palm (Palmae) Phoenix canariensis also called the Canarian date palm, originates from the Canary Islands, where it forma a up to 20 meter high tree. The feather formed leaves can be up to 5 meter long and 1 meter broad. The flowers comes in bunches and the fruit is small, dry and is noneateble.

The real date palm with eatable fruits is African, and is named Phoenix dactylifera doesn't grow in the Canary Islands.

The Canarian Scotch Pine (Pi´naceae) Pinus canariensis is a high stemmed and up to 30-meter-high tree. The young trees have a pyramid formed growth, while the old ones get a broader and rounder crown. The tree is very important for the Islands, among other things as water gatherer.

When the fog and the clouds are over the islands, than the endemic pines, which is a special kind with 3 long needles "on every leaf" is capable of catching the moisture and transform it to drops, which thereafter falls to earth. The cones are very big - 20 - 25 cm.

Pinus canariensis mostly grows in the higher areas, and the tree has a special gift to survive forest fires. At the same time, as the Europeans came to the island, there was too big a utilization of the pines among other things to furniture, balconies and more, on the islands and in Spain. From this utilization the Canaries lost about 80% of the pines on the islands.

Potatoes (Sola´naceae) Solanum tuberosum is a very important export article together with onions and tomatoes. In the Canary language one speaks of papa, and on castellan one talks of patata.

Because of the mild climate, it is possible to harvest twice a year, and it is the reason why the European markets has been customers outside their potato season. When the harvest on the European markets are plentiful the islands imports plants from Ireland and England.

Bayberries (Lau´raceae) Laurus canariensis. Here we are talking about a special Canarian kind, which by the way doesn't segregate much from the European Bay tree (Laurus nobilis) there might be a little less aroma in its leaves.

Heather (Eri´caceae) Erica arborea can reach up to 20 meter in height. The small white or pink flowers looks like the normal heather bushes on the moors in august. The roots of the heather trees is called bruyére tree, and its dark brown, very hard and fine kind of tree is used to produce pipe bowls

Onion (Liliáceae) Allium cepa grown in the islands is reckoned the most juicy and tasty in the world.

Almond tree (Ro´saceae) Prunus duchies, is a deciduous tree with an height of about 3 - 5 meter. which is grown many places on the islands, where there is sufficient water, special in the Barrancos. Its white and pink flowers gives a beautiful contrast to the barren stone landscape. It is flowering from the end of January / February.

Mango tree (Anacardiáceaea) Mangifera indica is a evergreen tree which originates from India, but gradually is spread in all tropical areas. Its tasty fruits are the size of apples, but are much more fibrous.

Mulberry tree (Mo´raceae) Morus Alba which originates from China is a deciduous tree. Earlier it was more spread than today. The few specimen left, reminds of a now disappeared silk industry. After the silkworm was imported to the Islands, the Canarian Engineer Augustin de Béthencourt y Molina in 1778, invented a silk spinning mill. But one couldn't stand against the artificial products.

Oleander (Apocy´naceae) Nerium Oleander is a evergreen bush, which can be up to 4 meter high. Oleander is everywhere on the Islands and is flowering with white, yellow. pink or red flowers.
Please Note, that the plants leaves and branches are very poisonous.

Orchilla (Roccella tinctoria) which maybe can be translated with colour-lichen, is a dry and stiff kind of lichen growing in tussocks high in the mountains and by difficult available coasts.

It is threaded and with a brown colour, which once in a while can look so dark, that it looks black. In-between there are white spots, and the highest plant is hardly more than 10 cm. For thousands of years this lichen has been used in the production of scarlet colours. Today the lichen is not exploited.

Papaya tree (Cari´caceae) Carica papaya, also called a melon-tree, originates from America and is a deciduous tree, which can reach 15 meter in height. It is cultivated a good many places in the Canary

Islands because of the tasty yellow fruits, which look a little like melons, but is tasting quite different. - something an orange and a threaded pear. Many is moistening the fruits in citron juice before they are eaten.

Thorn apple (Sola´naceae) Datura arborea is a small evergreen tree, often only a bush which many places is used as a ornamental plant. The bell-formed flowers in the night send out a penetrating smell.

The name Thorn apple is given because of the thorned fruit.
Please note, that all of the plant is very poisonous.

Senecio (Com'positae) Senecio kleinia has thick meaty stems with small lancet formed leaves, which often drops. They look a lot alike the leaves on an oleander.

Sugar cane (Gra´mineae) Saccharum officinarum was for hundreds of years the most important plant on the Canary Islands. It reached the islands by long and complicated roads, over among others India and China. Already in the beginning of the 16. century Portuguese sugar masters had the farmers growing the plants, which demanded much labour. That was why the negro slaves was imported to the islands, but the cultivating of sugar canes had much better climatically conditions in the West Indies, and it therefore was better to sell the slaves to the West Indian plantations, and that's why the Canary Islands haven't got a black population majority.

Sugar cane is still produced on the islands, but mainly to use in the production of rum

Column-Euphorbia (Euphorbi´acaae) Euphorbia canariensis. In Spanish it is called Cardón. It is a cactus like plant with stems of 2 meter height, covered by thorns. It's flowering in July and August with small red flowers.

Please note, that it's milky juice is poisonous.

Tamarisk (Tamari´caceae) Tamarix canariensis, which is the correct name, is the Bibles desert plant and is often seen on the dry islands as log-branched bushes with very small leaves and flowers. It is the principal food for camels, as it has been since Moses time in Sinai, Negev and Moab's desserts

Tomato (Sola´naceae) Lycopersicon is an important export article in the Canary Islands. The tomatoes is mainly cultivated in the southern areas in the low coast zones, and on the West coast around San Nicolas de Tolentino, where the valleys is covered with enormous greenhouses, and where a steady winter climate makes it possible lie a great part of the production to the winter months, where the request from Europe is the biggest. In total the export is about 300.000 tons.

Parks & Squares

Take a walk in the streets of any town in Gran Canaria and enjoy the many beautiful buildings and places. There are more sedate parks and places to discover, some right in the heart of Las Palmas, which is the bustling city of Gran Canaria and the most exciting city in all the Canary Islands.

Walk through the lovely parks in the island and soak up the nice atmosphere. Enjoy the marvellous nature surrounding the cities. There's an abundance of Spanish way of life here though, it's a city with almost 600 years of history and hasn't shrugged off much of that typically Spanish tradition. Relax on a street side cafe and watch the people passing by.

Gran Canaria is an island of festivities that continue throughout the year. There is not a town, village or country hamlet that does not celebrate its own special event, where nobody feels left out. It is precisely during these festivities when the innate hospitality and friendliness of the people of Gran Canaria become manifest.

These festivities also demonstrate the vitality, ambiguity and plurality of the elements and cultures in which the local population has been steeped for many centuries.

Below please find some of the greatest and most known parks and squares on Gran Canaria:

Parque Urbano de San Juan

Professor Lucas Arencibia

25200 Telde Gran Canaria

One of the largest parks on the whole of the Canary Islands, Gran Canarias Parque Urbano de San Juan is a particularly appealing location, situated in the Telde area. Covering 135000 square metres, this is the second largest urban park in the whole of the Canary Islands. Since it was finished, it has become the symbol of Telde as a town for the 21st century.

Highlights here include sculptures, walking and cycle trails devoted to Placido Fleitas, an artist from Telde, nature and woodland walks, a playground area for children, a large lake around the San Juan cemetery, open expanses of grass, outdoor concerts and seasonal events.

Opening hours:
Monday - Sunday 10.00 - 22.00
Admission: Free

Parque de San Telmo

Bravo Murillo

35003 Las Palmas

Heading out of Triana is Parque de San Telmo, with its shelter and bandstand, and the bus station, where you can get a bus to anywhere on the island.

This little haven of peace is located in the centre of the big city of Las Palmas, next to Calle Triana, with an abundance of different shops, restaurants and bars. This large park features sitting areas, pathways, mature landscaping with large palm trees and many popular outdoor events and activities, including a number of local fairs. It currently covers 17300 square metres.

Opening hours:
Monday - Sunday 24 hours
Admission: Free

Parque de Santa Catalina
Porte Las Palmas
35007 Las Palmas

In the middle of Las Canteras in the west and the harbour in the east, you find this beautiful park. A lot of the festivities, events and concerts that take place in the city, is located in this park. The carnival (February/march), for example, has it's main stage here, and the park is full of people.

It's a good place to start your sightseeing of Las Palmas, as many tourist buses have their stops here,

In the park you can see a sculpture, placed there by the City, of an old woman feeding the animals. She was actually an old homeless woman living in the park, and her name was Lolita Pluma. Pluma means feather, and she was called like this because she always had plenty of feathers on her from the birds she was feeding

In the streets around the park are many nice cafés, bars, restaurants and shops. Close to the Elder Museum of Science and Technology, the Parque de Santa Catalina is known for hosting many of the area's most notable carnivals and festivals.

Located next to La Luz and Las Palmas Ports, this park's wide central area is surrounded by the Science Museum, the Elder Building, a playarea for children and a modern tourist office.

Opening hours:
Monday - Sunday 24 hours
Admission: Free

Casa y Jardines de la Marquesa
(Marchioness of Arucas House and Gardens)
Carretera de Banaderos
35400 Arucas

Situated on the northern side of Gran Canaria, in the Arucas area, are the Casa y Jardines de la Marquesa, the house and gardens of the Marchioness of Arucas, owned by the person of the same name. Built in the late 19th century, this historic house features beautifully landscaped gardens and contains many outstanding botanical specimens.

However, although the house is lovely, the Romantic gardens are the most attractive feature of this property, and have been declared by the Canary Islands government to be worth conserving because of their aesthetic and botanical interest. This romantic 19th century garden is set in lavish plantations of banana and strelitzia.

There is a grotto, an exotic summer house, statues and many rare plants, and there are examples of tropical and subtropical flora in these gardens.

Opening hours:
Monday - Saturday
09.00 - 13.00 and 14.00 - 18.00
Admission: 5 €

Parque Doramas
(Pueblo Canario)
35005 Las Palmas

Parque Doramas is a beautiful park that lies in the district of Ciudad Jardin, in the middle of Vegueta and Las Canteras. The park is named after the guanche King Doramas, who fought against the Spanish for a long time, but in the end he was killed in Arucas.

After a day walking around in the city it is great to come here and relax. Sit down on one of the many benches, watch the water cascades and the statues, and explore the beautiful plants and flowers that you can find here.

Located in Parque Doramas is Pueblo Canario. This is a copy of a typical Canarian village. The Canarian painter Néstor de la Torre is the man behind this. Everything is artificial, but it is still a nice place to relax, buy souvenirs and local crafts, or look at traditional shows of dancing and singing.

A monument depicting aboriginal people tumbling over a precipice to escape capture symbolizes the resistance of the Guanche chief Doramas, after whom this park was named, against the Spanish invaders.

Doramas Park itself is a sub-tropical paradise in itself worth a visit. Cascading water features, abundant Canarian flora a terrace cafe and generally a world away from the surrounding city. In the centre of the park is THE hotel to be seen at, Hotel Santa Catalina. Dating back to the 1800s the original Canarian style of the building is quite spectacular and there's a nice terrace to sit out on for morning coffee or afternoon tea.

Gran Canaria is a great theme park itself as it has a large variety of leisure activities to offer the visitors. It has also developed some natural and artificial areas where it attractions and shows are put together just to entertain and in many cases to educate their visitors.

Although the island does not have large theme parks, places for leisure in Gran Canaria are noted for their variety, originality and a sense of being somehow linked to the surroundings and natural resources. Thus, you can find botanical gardens, zoos, water parks and those parks which are linked to the Canarian culture. You will also find scientific and amusement parks.

Beside the Parques mentioned we mustn't forget the Cactualdea Parque, Palmitos Parque and Botanic Garden, all of whom mentioned under Tour suggestions.

Smoking
Smoking on Gran Canaria
In force for many buildings and in all public means of transport on Gran Canaria there's a law restricting Smoking.

It will be more difficult to be a smoker in modern Spain. And it will be so much more difficult that it is important to all tourists to be orientated about how the law is build and how it functions. You are responsible about where you are smoking and the smokers will be fined too.

From January the 1st 2006 there has come a comprehensive smoking ban in Spain.

On November 8th 2005 the Spanish Congress unanimously approved a anti-tobacco Law. The new Law bans smoking in the workplace, the law prohibiting smoking indoors. The Law regulates all of the sale of Tobacco products in Spain.

More than 200 amendments to the Law was put forward during the reading of the Bill in Parliament, but only a few of these reached the final text.

The final wording of the Law, establish a total smoking ban:

- in public and private workplaces, smoking ban indoor
- in Health Centres, at Doctors and in Hospitals
- in schools and educational institutions
- in sports areas
- in public means of transport

- in business areas
- on service stations and in elevators

Selling of Tobacco to minors (persons under 18 years of age) is prohibited. Sale of Tobacco Products in public, administrative buildings and inclusive adjacent buildings, and in above mentioned areas is prohibited by Law.

Smoking will be permitted in special smoking areas in Airports and Bus terminals and in Theatres.

Bars and Restaurants can set up smoking areas, if they are clearly showed and is separated from the rest of the area. This separation is only necessary if the area is over 100 square meters.

Marketing of Tobacco Products in the Press, in the Radio, on advertising signs and in movie theatres, and promotional arrangements and free handing out of tobacco products is banned.

Offence against the Law will be punished with fines up to 600€, depending of the coarseness of the offence.

Hotels and Restaurants

The normal tourist will be fast to recognize, that a new Law has been put in force. But one thing is to recognize it. Something different is to decide ones attitude to the new Law.

Within the Branches of Restaurants and Hotels, the new Law holds many exceptions. Some of the exceptions leaves it up to the owner of the bar - or the restaurant, if you may smoke or not.

A bar under 100 square meters may in principle decide himself if it is to be a smokers bar or a non-smokers bar, they want to run. They have to show though that you may smoke, if it is a smokers bar. At the same time they have to be aware of that if it is a smokers bar/restaurant children is not allowed in.

That's why a tourist/visitor should realize the smoking policy of the particular public house.

Moreover it is decided by law, that all Hotels and serving places, in order to avoid misunderstandings, should have an easy understandable signing of the particular place's policy in this area, that is a display, telling where to smoke and where not to.

Why legislate in this area

O course there is a good health reason to a smoking ban, and that is PASSIVE SMOKING, and passive smoking has developed to being an important cause for European Authorities and certain of the Member-states of EU.

Passive smoking makes a sincere risk for the Health and for the Environment.

Passive smoking is what the non-smokers experiences when they inhale the tobacco smoke, others has exhaled into the surrounding air. The smoke comes from burning tobacco and from the air, a smoker exhales. Only 15% of the smoke from a cigarette is inhaled by the smoker - the rest of the smoke is spread to the surrounding air and can be inhaled by other persons present.

The tobacco-smoke contains more than 4000 chemical substances, where more then 50 is known for causing cancer, and more then 100 for being poisonous. Some of these substances is more concentrated in the smoke that is not inhaled, and that is one of the reasons why passive smoking is so dangerous.

And even if the Tobacco Industry denies it tremendously, much is indicating, that the additives in the tobacco also contains products, that is making it difficult to quit smoking.

Hands-on Information
Casino
For those looking to splash some cash, there are tree casinos on Gran Canaria, many of which belong to the big hotels.

Gran Casino Las Palmas

C/ Leon y Castillo 227

35006 Las Palmas

Tel. 928 23 39 08

This casino is situated within a 5-star hotel, the Santa Catalina, which means it has all the comforts you would expect from such a rating, including a magnificent restaurant and bar. The casino takes up a whole floor of the hotel, completely carpeted, decorated tastefully and with sophistication. There are elegant ceiling lamps and sofas with tables to have a drink. Typical games are played, like roulette, classic blackjack, poker, and slot machines. Entry is free, but there is a strict dress code.

Casino Palace

C/ Las Retamas 3, San Agustin

35100 San Bartolomé de Tirajana

Tel. 928 76 27 24

This is a Las Vegas-style casino in the Hotel Meliá Tamarindos where you can enjoy a full range of traditional gaming activities including Black Jack, French roulette, American roulette and even slot machines. There's also a gala dinner combined with a variety show featuring acts like international ballet companies, magicians and ice-skaters. Formal evening dress is recommended. Entry is free

Gran Casino Costa Meloneras

C/ Mar Mediterráneo 1, Meloneras

35510 San Bartolomé de Tirajana

Tel. 928 14 85 21

The third casino is located in Meloneras situated in the south of Gran Canaria, in the resort of Costa Meloneras, it stands directly on the beach front, giving fantastic views of the famous Maspalomas lighthouse and the ocean. The Meloneras beach and the natural dunes park of Maspalomas are both only a few minutes away on foot.

Gran Casino Costa Meloneras are located in an annexed building to the Hotel Costa Meloneras, and the Casino count on 17 tables, that they include plasma screens, where will be been the development of the plays, 100 vending machine and a "Mystery Jackpot", among other things.

The Great Casino Costa Meloneras also will make available of its visitors a hall spectacles, call "Black & Red Casino Show", a denominated restaurant "the Cupola of the Casino" and a modern Convention center.

Electricity

As in England the electricity runs on a 220 volt, 2 pin plug, so UK travellers usually need only bring a 2 pin "Southern Europe" adapter. On one occasion our accommodation required "Northern Europe" adapters, so it's probably wise to bring both.

Police

In Spain there are 3 different types of Police:

Policia Local is the local Police, and is placed under the local cities. Their task is among other things to direct the Traffic, and they are recognised on their blue Uniforms, and their cars.

Policia Nacional is the State Police, a kind of investigating officers, who also use blue Uniforms.

Guardia Civil, which for the most part function as Traffic officers. They are easily recognised on their Olive Green Uniforms, and the Green/White Cars with the Guardia Civil mark.

They are often placed in Roundabouts, where it is easy to see, if people are using the safety belts. Remember them!

Furthermore they takes care of narcotics and illegal refugees.

And they is also driving in civil cars and are wearing civilian clothes.

Telephone numbers is found under the cities.

(If it is an emergency, Policia Local - 092, and Guardia Civil - 062.)

Post Offices

Post Offices are generally open Monday to Friday 08.30 - 13.30 and 09.30 - 13.00 on Saturdays

Mail to England is normally 4 - 7 days in reaching the receiver.

Spanish Postage rates		
Weight	To Spain	To Europe
till 20 g (standard format)	0,29 €	0,57 €
till 20 g (other formats)	0,38 €	1,05 €
21-50 g	0,41 €	1,26 €
51-100 g	0,57 €	1,44 €
101-200 g	0,93 €	2,91 €
201-350 g	1,65 €	5,45 €
351-1000 g	3,24 €	9,09 €
1001-2000 g	3,91 €	15,95 €

English	Spanish

Address	Dirección
Envelope	Sobre
Letter	Carta
Letter Box	Buzón
Mail	Correo
Parcel	Paquete
Post	Correo
Post code	Codigo postal
Post Office	Oficina de correos
Postcard	Tarjeta postal
Postman	Cartero
Receive	Recibir
Recipient	Receptor
Registered mail	Correo registrado
Return address	Direccion del remitente
Send	Enviar
Sender	Remitente
Stamp	Sello

Telephone

International telephone calls can be made from almost anywhere in the Canary Islands. The distinctive blue booths are not easily missed. You have the choice of using coins, phone cards (tarjetas telefónicas) and sometimes credit cards.

www.telephoneguiden.com
The country code for Gran Canaria is the same as for Spain (0034) followed by a nine digit number usually starting with 928. Telephone calls made from bars, restaurants and hotels are usually a great deal more expensive than the street pay booths.

The cheap rate for international calls is the night tariff from 22.00 to 08.00 hours and all day Sunday.

Theft

As everywhere in the world: when there are many tourists, there are many pick pockets. Every day handbags and purses are stolen, and a good advice is, to keep your handbag close to your body, and never have your purse in your back pocket.

Never let your values be on the beach, when going in the water. Remember to lock the car, and don't let anything valuable lie on the seats, so a thief can be tempted.

It often happens in connection with arrival and departure in the airport and where many people are gathered on market places and so on. Therefore pay special attention on such places.

Another evident subject for a thief is the hotel room, so remember to close windows and doors - even when you are home. Saying home we also mean in the night, because a thief isn't afraid of going in, while you are sleeping.

What to do, if your things are stolen abroad!

If you are robbed abroad, you have to notify the local police. Address and telephone number is to be found under the city you live in. It's an assumption for you to, if your insurance company are to pay for your stolen goods. Therefore get a copy of the notification/police report with you home.

Stolen Credit cards

If your Credit Card is stolen, you have to call your bank at once, and maybe to the credit card company to have your stolen card blocked. Read under banks.

Stolen Passport

If you loose your Passport, the Embassy in Madrid or one of the Consulatesspread around Spain issue a provisory Passport, valid to your homecoming to England. Before that can take place, you have to go to the local police and notify the loss of the passport, and ask for a police report "denuncia policial". The police report is brought to the Embassy/Consulate included two photos in the passport size (3,5 x 4,5 cm). When receiving a provisory passport, you have to pay a fee - see the section concerning fees,

Stolen air ticket

If your air ticket is stolen, you have to contact the air company at once. If you are able to prove, that you have ordered and paid for it, the Travel Agency or the Air Company can issue an emergency ticket. Under normal conditions your name will often be in the computer system, so you are able to document the reservation by showing your passport. In order to receive a new ticket, you have to sign a "solemn declaration", wherein you promise to pay for the disappeared ticket, if it is used before it is expired. By the way isn't it free of charge to have a new ticket issued. It is fairly expensive, maybe 50 - 75 €.

Anything else

Your normal insurance will as a rule cover your loss by theft. There will be some restrictions. As an example will theft of cash normally be covered by a much smaller amount.

Tourist Office
Tourist Information Offices

Gran Canaria has an extensive network of tourist information offices that are situated in every city and town on the island. Here, visitors can obtain information on everything that they may wish to know about the island's culture, customs, places of interest, etc. Find tourist information under each cities.

Water

There are 2 water systems on the Island. "Main water" is supplied by local authorities and is used for the houses in towns and villages. "Natural water" is also used in country areas in the houses and on the land. Tourists are advised to buy bottled water.

And here's a very good tip: Cold water (drink) out of the fridge might seem refreshing and will cool you down, but it is important to realise, that it can have the opposite effect. Your body becomes cooler where the water reaches and its automatic reaction is to compensate for this by trying to warm your body up!

Natural water

There is a network of pipes, gullies and tanks on the island which brings the natural 'spring' water from the higher altitudes to farms, towns and villages on the lower parts of the island. The quality of the water is excellent, but the quality of pipes and tanks may not always be so good.

The water here is safe to use for washing food and cleaning your teeth and so on but bad stomachs do tend to be a problem here, although I strongly believe that's linked to the low price of alcohol. Drink bottled water. Ice cubes in bars and restaurants are made from bottled water too, so are safe to consume.

Tap water
The quality of the tap water varies from area to area. Water (in a few towns (areas)) can be drunk from the tap, but to be sure, check by the authorities. The quality of the water in the towns can vary from week to week. The usual chemicals are added.

Bottled water - still
Agua sin gas: There are several companies on the island that bottle the spring water and distribute it to shops, supermarkets, cafes and restaurants. It comes in plastic containers or glass bottles varying from 100 ml to 8 litres. Always take a bottle with you if you go walking or driving.

Bottled water - aerated
Agua con gas: This is the same as the "still water" but with bubbles added.

A very big part of the drinking water on this Island, originates in Aqua's de Firgas.

ESA - Space Agency
INTA Estacion Espacial de Maspalomas
Apartado 29, 35100 Maspalomas
Tel. 928 72 71 00
Fax. 928 72 71 24

The Maspalomas ground station is located approximately 38 kilometres from Gran Canaria International Airport and 60 kilometres from the city of Las Palmas de Gran Canaria. Transport between the airport and the station is by rental car or taxi. Take the motorway south from the airport.

When you have passed Playa del Inglés (on your left) you will see mountains, with a lot of

big antennas and paraboles, directed towards space. That is the INTA Estacion Espacial de Maspalomas, that is part of ESA, the European Space Agency.

ESA have a lot of things to do. The survey almost all spaceship movements, European as well as American, and a lot of satellites are monitored by ESA. Right now there are about 18 satellites being monitored. And they are travelling far. Som go to other planets in our solar system, and some are going further.

GMES (Global Monitoring for Environment and Security) is the next flagship initiative for space in Europe, after Galileo.

It was confirmed as the European Union's priority at the 2001 Summit in Gothenburg, where the Heads of State and Government requested that "the Community contribute to establishing by 2008 a European capacity for Global Monitoring for Environment and Security".

ESA is the main partner to the European Union in GMES and has contributed with programmatic activities since 2001 to the GMES endeavour. ESA has worked on the development of GMES pilot services in close conjunction with a large community of operational users.

ESA is also working on multi-mission facilities and ground segment operations and is preparing the Space Component for GMES with a series of studies and preparatory activities for the development of a series of satellites missions (the Sentinels) and the integration of national and European missions to guarantee continuity of data and services.

GMES is the response to the need by Europe for geo-spatial information services. It provides autonomous and independent access to information for policy-makers, particularly in relation to environment and security.

GMES represents also the European contribution to the international Global Earth Observation System of Systems, GEOSS, which was established at the third Earth Observation Summit in Brussels, in February 2005.

And be sure, if anything happens in space, ESA is among the first to know, and one of the means to this is the Station in Maspalomas.

Holidays

Christmas

In Spain Christmas Eve is called: Noche Buena - The good Night!

The family Christmas Eve meal is one of the most important meals of the year for a Spanish family and the housewife will be busy preparing the traditional fare. It could be Turkey, but it is often fish.

As Christmas candy the Spaniards are eating "Turron" a kind of assorted chocolate, produced of among other things almonds and honey, or maybe marzipan. The meal will be complimented with champagne, and preferably the Spanish "Cava".

After the meal the adults will then exchange presents. The children will usually only receive a small gift. At midnight, some people will go to the Midnight Mass at the church. Others may stay at home and open a bottle of champagne to celebrate the birth of Christ.

Some children go Carol singing and the youngsters may go to bed whilst the adults go out and party until dawn.

Christmas Day is a fiesta day so all banks and shops are closed, probably to recover from the night before. Christmas Day in Spain is one of the quietest of the year. Anyone wanting to eat out on this special day will have to book well in advance.

The first major sign of Christmas is the state-run lottery which is drawn on December 22nd. The 'El Gordo' (the Fat One) is one of the largest lotteries in the world and thousands of people win each year.

In general, Christmas in Spain is based more on a religious theme than in many other places. Churches are packed to capacity, day and night.

Spain has many of its own unique traditions, all of which are great fun, but many of the Spanish traditions, are the same in the former Spanish colonies. In Spain there are many Christmas markets through

December. Many parties are celebrated in the different cities during these markets.

Traditionally it is the Twelfth Night (the 6th of January), where the Holy 3 Kings - Los Reyes Magos (Melchor, Gaspar and Balthazar) that is bringing the gifts in Spain. It is namely on this day, that you'll receive your Christmas gifts, as a symbol on the arrival of the Holy Three Kings at the Crib of the Infant Jesus.

The evening before, the 5th of January, there are parades in most cities, where the Kings are riding through the cities on Camels, horses, donkeys or in decorated vans or busses. In the evening all the children place their footwear outside the door, before going to bed. The next morning the Holy 3 Kings have placed presents in them. The most bellowed is Balthazar.

New Year

New Years Eve - Noche Vieja:

New Years Eve - Noche Vieja is celebrated with festivity. It is very normal to go to a restaurant, and here you normally buy an entire arrangement.

Are you in Spain on New Years Eve, then make your reservations as early as possible, as New Year's Eve is very big here. Most bars and restaurants are open for private parties only, and many towns organise street parties with entertainment and firework displays that last all night. For most Spaniards it is a night for going out and for fireworks.

At the stroke of midnight it is tradition to eat 12 grapes - one on each stroke of the clock, to bring good luck for the new year. On New Year's Eve, Noche Vieja (which translates better to Old Year's Night), or San Silvestre in Spain.

Celebrations revolve around the eating of grapes. The idea is to eat 12 grapes at midnight, one grape on each stroke of the clock, for luck. It is difficult to do, so you'd better be ready to wash it down with Cava.

New Year in Spain is announced on Television via the twelve chimes at midnight from the Puerta del Sol in Madrid. An hour later in the Canaries with those of the Cabildo in Las Palmas on Gran Canaria.

Carnival

Almost all places in Gran Canaria celebrate their carnival. The most important are the carnival of Las Palmas de Gran Canaria, Playa del Inglés, Arguineguín, Agüimes, Agaete and Telde, each of them with a characteristic flavour and the participation of a great number of people.

The Carnival linked to the Easter season begins around the end of February and sees festivities across the island, with particular emphasis on the towns of Las Palmas, San Bartolomé, Maspalomas, Agüimes, Agaete and Telde, with each town having its own specific events during this period (February/March). Processions, singing groups competition, musical bands, carnival queens.

There are other colourful festivities, for instance Maspalomas Carnival - in mid-May, a colourful gay and lesbian carnival around the Playa del Inglés area of Gran Canarias's Maspalomas resort, with Carnival Queen and Drag Queen contests, together with parades and many events focused on the Yumbo Shopping Centre.

Immigration

Moving

Moving to Gran Canaria - Checklist
Learn Spanish, and if you have children, get them learning Spanish as soon as possible too. Moving to a new country, changing schools and making new friends will be hard enough for them as it is.

Choose an area to live in. You may want to move to somewhere where you will be able to speak English if you have to - if that is the case, choose somewhere near the coast, or near a major inland tourist area such as Playa del Inglés or Puerto Rico in the south of the island. It can be more interesting to live somewhere more typically Gran Canaria though - you need to research as much as you can.

If you own your house. Decide whether you want to sell it and live on the capital for a while, or if you want to rent it out while you decide what to do. The latter option is generally the safest, but either way, you should talk to some local estate agents and start to make arrangements.

Plan your move. If you have children, then summer is a good time to move to Gran Canaria as most schools will not accept new pupils mid-year. In fact you may want to move in May/June, so that you have the best chance of securing a place in the school of your choice for the following September. If you are planning to find a long-term rental property, then book 2 or 3 weeks in a hotel or apartment / villa either a month before your proposed moving date or immediately prior to it.

You are unlikely to be able to organise anything any further ahead than that, as properties tend to be rented out quickly on Gran Canaria.

Check whether your bank will allow you to keep your accounts once you live in Gran Canaria. If your bank does not allow it, move your account to one that does.

2 months before you go

Start to sort your belongings and sell or give away anything you do not want to keep. This always takes longer than you think it will!

If you are taking your car, get it MOT'd, and check whether your insurance covers driving in Gran Canaria.

Find an international removals company and buy some boxes (it is not worth trying to save money on boxes - you want the double thickness international freight ones).

1 month before you go

If you are British, then get the new E111 card.

Fill in form P85 and take it to your nearest tax office or your employer.

Unless you are moving to Gran Canaria in April, you should have a tax rebate to collect (since you can claim your full year's tax allowance).

Go to your bank and fill in a "Not ordinarily resident" form so that you will not pay tax on your savings - make sure you give them your new address.

Bank Account
Different types of Accounts

A Current account (cuenta corrente) usually carries a very low interest rate, if any. You can ask for a cheque book.

A fixed deposit account (cuenta de imposicion a plazo) will give you interest depending on the time period of the deposit and the amount deposited. Banks CAN be bargained with about these conditions.

A Savings book account (libreta de ahorro) also carries a low interest rate , but does give you a continuous record of your account and in some cases ca be used in cash machines for withdrawing money.

If you want to open a bank account on Gran Canaria, you will only need your passport or residence permit, and will be asked to fill out a form from the bank which will also set out the banks general terms and conditions. You will also be asked for your NIE number.

If you are not a resident, you will have to submit, apart from the documents proving your identity, a certificate of non-resident issued by a Police Station. For the rest of the foreigners residents on Gran Canaria, there is no restriction regarding the opening of bank accounts.

Remember, anyway, that most banks provides their customers with a card that allows them to obtain cash, 24 hours a day, in the automatic cashiers network, spread all around the national territory.

Fiscal residents on Gran Canaria can open a current and savings account for residents. Non-residents can only open current and savings account for non- residents.

Please note that it is in your own interest as far as the banking system goes, to become a resident as soon as possible concerning tax liabilities, charges & interest go.

Commissions and services vary greatly among the banks, so compare several, and make a decision based on your needs. As often on Gran Canaria, and everywhere else, a personal relationship at a bank is really helpful for sorting out problems, if you need to get anything non-standard done.

Ask friends, colleagues or teachers if they can introduce you to a director or sub-director of a local branch. If you have an opportunity take advantage of it.

Fees & services

In terms of fees and services, non-resident accounts are virtually the same as resident ones.

The only differences being, that the bank may not be willing to issue you a credit card or provide you overdraft protection. Should the bank charge significantly higher fees for being a non-resident, we would recommend taking your business elsewhere.

One final word of caution regarding opening accounts: if you make the initial deposit in a foreign currency, be sure to specifically ask that the currency be converted into euros immediately (we have heard of cases where this became a problem later).

The bank should charge you no more than their typical foreign exchange commissions for this operation.

The Spanish banks runs a convenient system called *domiciliación* that allows companies to directly debit your account for billing purposes.

Phone and utility companies are big users of this system; many of them actually require you to pay in this manner.

In case you choose not to pay your bills through this route, you will have to go to a bank anyway to pay it person (not necessarily your bank either). The hours for making these payments are fairly restricted, usually between 8:30 and 10:30 and sometimes only on certain days of the week (one example is Monday, Wednesday, Friday).

The bank is obliged to retain 18% of the interest you earn but not on a fixed deposit by a non- resident. The bank should also prepare a statement giving your average balance for the year to be used in your wealth tax return.

Transfer of Funds.

There are now no restrictions on transferring funds to and from Spain from other countries of the European Union and the ESS.

However if you want to take out more than 13,353 euros from Spain to another country , or move more than 80,000 euros within Spain, you are obliged to communicate it with the authorities, which the bank will also advise you on.

If you want to make transfers to or from countries outside the EU area, you need to consult you own bank.

Some banks are still charging heavy commissions on transfers of pensions from abroad while other banks do not so it is advisable to "shop" around.

The EU has decided to eliminate the commissions when using cash machines outside your own country, but inside the EU area......At last!

The Cheque on Gran Canaria.

Write cheques only in ball point pen or ink. Write (or accept) a cheque to the person or business that is to receive payment and not to the bearer (al portador).

To ensure that a cheque can only be deposited into the account of the person or business to whom it is made, write to be credited to the account of (a abonar en cuenta) before the name of the recipient, or cross the cheque with two parallel lines.

Do not leave blank spaces, which could be used to increase the amount. Keep blank cheques, destroy excess cheques, and never leave a blank signed cheque for anyone. Writing a cheque without funds in the bank is illegal.

Bank Statements.

Most banks are willing to send your statements to any address you want whether on Gran Canaria or your home country.

The identifying number is the same as on your cheques with the first four digits giving the banks number , the next four the branch number then two control numbers and the last ten your own account number.

Gestoria

A gestor is a concept that many foreigners, new to Spain, have trouble understanding as the profession simply does not exist in their home countries. Gestors came into being because traditionally

the bureaucracy in Spain was complicated (and to large degree continues to be).

In other words, the Gestor is a profession dedicated principally to helping you with Spanish Bureaucracy. Luckily there are many English speaking Gestors in the popular costal towns on hand to help.

Every Spanish town has at least one Gestor. They are a necessary part of life because Spanish government and council officials are notoriously slow and nit-picking. Bureaucratic procedures are archaically complex and have to be slavishly followed to the letter.

However, rather than single-handedly wrestling with these bureaucrats you can sit back and let a Gestor do the slog for you. A Gestor is generally efficiently attentive to there's clients and the fees are normally very reasonable. Gestors are professionals and also belong to a Colegio.

Gestor is a general purpose consultant who can make your life in Spain much easier. Working in an office known as a Gestoría, they acts as an intermediary in your relations with the various official bodies. They knows the workings of many council and local government corridors and is usually able to obtain an official permit or document far quicker than you could on your own even if you were fluent in Spanish.

Warning

Although a Gestor will advise you on what you can claim and what you should not claim when completing any income or allowance sections of a form, remember it is you who signs the form at the end of the day and you are responsible for your own declaration.

Be aware that a Gestor is not a Lawyer or a Tax Consultant and in certain specialist areas it may be necessary to seek the advice of these more qualified professionals.

Services

If you are not resident in Spain, then a Gestor will make sure that the bills get paid and that your home is still there and waiting for you when you return.

The average Spaniard would not consider trying to obtain certain permits and licences without using a Gestor. So why try to survive without using a Gestor?

Typically, a Gestor will be able to handle the following matters for you:

Taxes	Administration of income and wealth tax for residents and non-residents alike. Payment of local taxes such as rates (IBI), rubbish, and car tax for Spanish vehicles.
Conveyancing	A Gestor can handle all of the legal work and tax payments required for a property purchase or sale.
Vehicles	They can arrange for change of ownership and addresses to be registered, as well as helping with paperwork involved in obtaining a Spanish driving license and importing vehicles.
Business	If you decide to set up a business, then a Gestor will offer essential advice on preparing employment contracts and paying social security contributions.
NIE residency	A Gestor can help you obtain a residency permit. They can also arrange for your national foreigner identification number (NIE) to be issued. You will need this number after buying a local property.
Insurance	Many Gestors are insurance agents and can arrange insurance for your life, house, and car.
Wills	Your Gestor can give you advice on preparing a will for your Spanish property, as well as liaising with the local notary for the signing of the will.
Permits	Your Gestor can also arrange for your fishing and hunting licenses to be issued as well as a gun license.

In addition to the above you will find your local Gestor a source of information and practical advice for resolving the various administrative problems that appear in everyday life

Residencia / NIE

Information on residing on Gran Canaria

Gran Canaria is an island, where it is necessary to have your paperwork in order, and to the correct paperwork comes the correct Identification numbers.

Information on how to get your NIE number, social security number and other forms of identification, will be told in this article, so please pay attention.

Whether you become a resident on Gran Canaria or remain non-resident, it is important to know, that if you have financial affairs in Spain, i.e. ownership of property, a tax identification number is a must.

DNI: (Documento Nacional de Identidad): This is the ID number for Spanish citizens. The same number is used for one's driver's license.

NIF: (Número de Identificación Fiscal): This is the tax ID number for all individuals. For all Spaniards, it's the DNI plus one letter; for foreigners, it's the same number as your NIE. Once you have an NIE, you do not need to re-apply for an NIF; if and when you have to pay taxes, use your NIE number. If you're a non-resident who has to pay taxes in Spain, you may get an NIF issued to you without having an NIE. This, of course, does not mean you get automatic residency in Spain, nor will it make it any easier to get residency.

CIF: (Certificado de Identificación Fiscal): This is the the same as the NIF, but for companies.

Non-Spanish residents have a tax reference number referred to as a "NIE" or "Numero de Identification Extranjero"

NIE: (Numero Identificacion Extranjeros): The immigration service issues this number to you once you obtain residency (you will find the number on your Resident Card). This is your identification number in Spain, and it is unique to you. You will need to take a photocopy of the important pages of your passport, and bring them as well, until you have your residency card. The NIE number is needed in order to file taxes, open a bank account (you don't have to, if it's foreign accounts), establish a business, and for almost any other form you fill out. Both EU citizens and non-EU citizens get issued an NIE number.

An NIE number is essentially a tax number for foreigners in Spain. You need one if you are going to buy a house or a car, if you want to apply for residencia or are going to work for a Spanish company. To get an

NIE number, you need to go to the extranjeros department at your nearest Comisaria (The police station for Policia Nacional, not the Policia Local). You can get a Gestor to apply for you, but it will cost you about 100 €. To do it your self, go to the National Police station in Maspalomas and collect an application form. This is a simple process providing you follow the guidelines. You will need to take your passport. The forms are fairly straightforward and you will have your NIE number within 2-6 weeks of applying.

HOW TO FILL IN THE N.I.E. APPLICATION FORM

1 DATOS PERSONALES   Means PERSONAL DETAILS

1er Apellido:	Surname
2º Apellido:	(Second Surname) Write chiffons instead (---)
Nombre:	First Name (Make sure to use same as in passport)
Fecha de Nacimiento:	Date of birth (Use two digits for day and month)
Lugar de nacimiento:	Place of birth
Sexo:	Gender "H" for Male (Hombre) and "M" Female (Mujer). X cross the one applicable
Estado Civil:	Status. S for single C for married. V for widow and D for divorced

País de nacimiento:	Country of Birth
País de nacionalidad:	Current Nationality
Nombre del padre:	Father's name (Also if dead)
Nombre de la madre:	Mother's name (Also if dead)
Domicilio en España:	Address in Spain (If you have one, otherwise leave blank)
Localidad:	Town
CP:	Postcode
Provincia:	Province

2)

Reasons for application:

Economic, Professional or Social (Tick professional for work reasons or social for house purchase)

3)

DOMICILIO A EFECTOS DE NOTIFICACIONES

Leave blank

Sign the form at the bottom, under 'Firma de solícitante'.

Complete the form and take it back to the National Police station, along with a photocopy. You also need to provide your original passport and a photocopy. That's it! You will then be told to return in approx. 4 weeks time when your number will be ready to collect. You need this number to do anything fiscal in Spain such as open a bank account. (This can also be done with your passport number).

Inspection Motorcars
Inspección Téchnica de Vehículos
I T V
Technical inspection on motorcars

After the age of four years, it will be necessary to have the vehicle undertake a safety test, generally known as an ITV in Spain (similar to an MOT in the UK). This must be undertaken every two years. When the vehicle is 10 years, the safety test is due every year.

The vehicle must be taken to a ITV station where a series of checks will be made to ensure, that the car meets the safety standards required to use the roads in Spain.

Many garages will, for a fee, check your vehicle and even take it to the ITV station for you.

Once the ITV is passed you will be issued with a certificate, the original of which must be kept in your vehicle in case the police stop you and wish to inspect it.

Failures under the test will be listed on a separate sheet and you will be allowed 15 days in which to get the faults repaired and have a re-test.

Insurance

1. General information

Insurance is a contract relationship entered into by the insurer and the insured. Such a contract, more commonly called the policy, usually provides that, on payment of the premium, the insurer promises to indemnify and reimburse the insured for any loss incurred by him from certain stated causes.

The policy, as a contract, must contain all of the elements necessary for a valid contract. The mutual considerations here are the premium paid by the insured and the promise of coverage made by the insurance company.

The causes of damage as provided for in the policy are also called "risks". The company specifically stipulates those risks which are covered under the particular policy. Any risk that is not stated shall not be included.

A policy must have a subject which is to be insured. It may be the life of a designated person, a house…

The risk or peril against which the life or property is to be insured must be specified in the policy: the death of a person, liability resulting from the negligent operation of an automobile…

The amount for which the policy covers the loss must be indicated.

The insurance taker is the holder of the policy. Normally the term during which the policy will be in effect is 1 year, after which it is renewed automatically unless you decide not to renew it, in which case you should previously advise the insurance company 2 months before it is due.

2. Proposal for insurance

Your application for an insurance do not oblige you to finally contract it. On the contrary, the insurance company is bound by the terms and conditions of its proposal for insurance for a term of 15 days.

3. Cancellation

An **insurance company** may cancel an insurance policy only under the following circumstances:

- ➢ If the insured has lied or made false statements on his/her application or in a claim he/she submitted.
- ➢ If the peril covered is increased. In these cases when there is no good faith, the insurance company shall pay the difference between the premium agreed and the premium which should have been paid for the increase of the risk.
- ➢ If the insured object is sold.
- ➢ Failure to pay premiums when they fall due, there is a 30-day grace period available to the insured to give him an opportunity to pay the premium without affecting his rights under the policy.

An insured may cancel an insurance policy in the event that the insurance company refuses to modify the policy when the new circumstances arisen can make the premium reduced. The policyholder is entitled to a refund calculated as the difference between the premium paid and the premium which should have been paid since the peril reduction was noticed.

4. In case the insured event occurs

If the insured event occurs, the policy taker or the beneficiary shall notify the insurance company within 7 working days, unless other period is stated in the insurance contract. Failure to give timely notice can result in an indemnification for the insurance company.

The assured must furnish a list of the items lost or damaged. The insurance company will investigate it and value the damages, it shall pay an indemnity or repair the insured object.

The insurance company shall pay part of the indemnity within 40 days from notice of loss, full indemnification shall be paid within 3 months from the notification date.

The insurance company may not pay the indemnity if it feels that the policyholder engaged in some type of misconduct which voided the coverage.

5. Complaining before the Spanish judge authorities

If the insurance company won't pay the claim or won't pay what the insured think the claim is worth, the insured may file a lawsuit against the insurance company. The type of court procedure will depend upon the amount to be claimed: either ordinary court procedure (*juicio ordinario*), or oral court procedure (*juicio verbal*) can be taken.

The period of time within to file the lawsuit will be:

- **2 years**, from the date of the report of the event, if the insurance only covered material damages (property insurance or car insurance), or

- **5 years**, from the date of the report of the event, if the insurance covered personal injuries (life or medical insurance). The insured may also claim before the General Insurance Office (*Dirección General de Seguros*).

Because of the complexity of insurance policies and because the resolution of coverage disputes often depends on careful analysis of the circumstances of the case, the assistance of an experienced Spanish Lawyer is strongly advisable.

6. Types of insurance

6.1. Homeowner's insurance

The homeowner's insurance (*seguro del hogar*) covers your house, the home itself and the things you keep in it against disasters: fire, wind...

The premium of the policy will depend on the value of the house, the things you keep in it and the risks you wish to be covered.

While a house is rented, it may only be insured by the landlord, the tenant may insure its content.

There is no law that requires a homeowner to have insurance, however, if you borrow money to buy a house, the bank will normally require you to contract, at least, a fire insurance to protect its interest until the loan is repaid.

6.2. Life insurance

A contract of life insurance (*seguro de vida*) provides that, in consideration of the premium to be paid, the insurer promises to pay the beneficiary an agreed sum upon the death of the person whose life is to be insured.

The person whose life is insured is generally called the "insured". The person named in the policy to benefit from the death of that person is called the "beneficiary". Where the policy contains the identity of the beneficiaries, they will not have to wait for the estate partition to be made in order to perceive the indemnity.

The insurance company normally requires a medical exam from people who are applying for life insurance.

The company may specifically exclude certain coverage, such as the coverage of death by suicide.

6.3. Health insurance

In this case the insurer agrees to pay to the insured a stipulated sum in the event of illness or temporary disability, as well as cover the cost of medical assistance.

There are two types of health insurance:

- ➢ Medical assistance: The insurance companies have a wide range of doctors who may assist you. The coverage will depend upon the terms agreed in the policy.
- ➢ The reimbursement of expenses for medical assistance: in this case you choose the doctor, the insurance company shall return the medical expenses to you within certain limits.

The health insurance does not cover some specific situations such as the hospitalization in case of transmissible diseases (AIDS), medical treatment for alcoholism, addiction to drugs, labor accidents ...

Frequently the insurance companies do not admit insurances for persons aged over 60 years old, in case they admit them, the policy cost will be increased.

Coverage period is for 1 year, the policy costs are increased every year.

6.4. Automobile Insurance

Insurance in Spain relating to automobiles can be divided into 2 categories:

- ➢ Third party liability insurance (seguro de terceros o de responsabilidad civil obligatoria)
- ➢ Full comprehensive insurance coverage (Seguro a todo riesgo)

6.4.1. Third party liability insurance

The third party liability insurance (*seguro de terceros o de responsabilidad civil obligatoria*) is mandatory in Spain. It is the minimum insurance required by Spanish law to drive a vehicle in Spain.

It covers the risk for causing personal injury and damage on third party's property (driver and passengers in another car with which it collided, passengers on the car who are not members of the insured family, pedestrians...).

The maximum indemnity this type of insurance covers is:

- ➢ In case of personal injury: € 336,566.78 per victim
- ➢ In case of property damage: € 96,161.94 per victim

In case of personal injury, the responsible for the accident will not be obliged to pay indemnity when proving that the injuries resulted from the injured party negligent operation or from force majeure.

This type of insurance does not cover:

- Personal injury of the insurance taker, the driver or the owner of the insured car.
- The damage caused to the insured vehicle, the things it kept in it, personal property of the insurance taker, the driver, the owner of the insured car and the spouse and relatives.

This type of insurance will not cover the damages caused in any of the following cases:

- If the driver were under the influence of drugs or alcohol.
- Where the vehicle is driven by a person that the owner did not authorize
- Where the driver does not have driving license

However, in any of these cases, the insurance company shall pay the corresponding indemnity to the injured party, which may be protested against the insurance taker.

Extra cover can be added to the insurance policy, driver and passenger insurance (seguro de ocupantes) is strongly recommended as the third party liability insurance does not cover the driver or his family and they must be insured separately.

6.4.2. Full comprehensive insurance coverage

The Full comprehensive insurance coverage (*Seguro a todo riesgo*) covers the injuries and damages non-covered in the third party liability insurance:

- The injuries to the insurance taker, the car owner, driver and the spouse, ascendants, descendants, relatives and the car passengers.
- Damages to the vehicle irrespective of how it is caused. This insurance also includes coverage against fire and breakage of glass.
- Damages of the car contents.
- Theft of the vehicle....

If the insured fails to pay the policy, he or she will have 5 months to pay it, when paid within this period of time, coverage will be recovered in 24 hours.

If you wish to contract an automobile insurance in Spain, it is advisable to bring proof of no claims from your previous insurance company, as this will help reduce your insurance premiums. If you have moved from another European country perhaps your old insurance company also operates in Spain, this might help you to get a better rate as they can check your claims history faster.

These are only general guidelines and not definitive statements of the law, all questions about the law's applications to individual cases shall be directed to aSpanish Lawyer.

School

Spanish Schools

The Spanish education system has changed dramatically over the last 10 years. Previously the system was elitist and secondary education was mostly private. University was out of the question for the majority of young people.

Today the story is very different. School attendance is now free and compulsory for all children between the ages of six and 15. Ninety-five per cent of children aged four to five are now in pre-school education and more than 55 per cent of children stay on at school until the age of 18.

The student body at universities now numbers over a million. It is interesting to note that female students now outnumber the males in secondary education and in the first years at university.

Spain has a state funded school system along with private schools and a range of international / foreign schools. Around 30% of Spain's' schoolchildren attend private schools the majority of which are co-educational.

The line between public, private and church schools can be blurred, with many nominally private or church schools receiving their principal support from the state.

International and foreign schools are the only schools which use English as the teaching language. If your children attend any other schools they will be taught their lessons in Spanish.

Attending a Spanish school, whether state or private, is probably the best way for your children to integrate into Spanish society. State schools have improved tremendously in recent decades and in general, are of a comparable quality with those in other EU countries, although the teaching methods used may differ.

If you are thinking of moving to Catalonia, the Balearics or the Basque region, remember to find out what language the schools teach in.

If you wish to contract an automobile insurance in Spain, it is advisable to bring proof of no claims from your previous insurance company, as this will help reduce your insurance premiums. If you have moved from another European country perhaps your old insurance company also operates in Spain, this might help you to get a better rate as they can check your claims history faster.

These are only general guidelines and not definitive statements of the law, all questions about the law's applications to individual cases shall be directed to aSpanish Lawyer.

School

Spanish Schools

The Spanish education system has changed dramatically over the last 10 years. Previously the system was elitist and secondary education was mostly private. University was out of the question for the majority of young people.

Today the story is very different. School attendance is now free and compulsory for all children between the ages of six and 15. Ninety-five per cent of children aged four to five are now in pre-school education and more than 55 per cent of children stay on at school until the age of 18.

Extra cover can be added to the insurance policy, driver and passenger insurance (seguro de ocupantes) is strongly recommended as the third party liability insurance does not cover the driver or his family and they must be insured separately.

6.4.2. Full comprehensive insurance coverage

The Full comprehensive insurance coverage (*Seguro a todo riesgo*) covers the injuries and damages non-covered in the third party liability insurance:

- ➤ The injuries to the insurance taker, the car owner, driver and the spouse, ascendants, descendants, relatives and the car passengers.
- ➤ Damages to the vehicle irrespective of how it is caused. This insurance also includes coverage against fire and breakage of glass.
- ➤ Damages of the car contents.
- ➤ Theft of the vehicle....

If the insured fails to pay the policy, he or she will have 5 months to pay it, when paid within this period of time, coverage will be recovered in 24 hours.

In case of personal injury, the responsible for the accident will not be obliged to pay indemnity when proving that the injuries resulted from the injured party negligent operation or from force majeure.

This type of insurance does not cover:

- Personal injury of the insurance taker, the driver or the owner of the insured car.
- The damage caused to the insured vehicle, the things it kept in it, personal property of the insurance taker, the driver, the owner of the insured car and the spouse and relatives.

This type of insurance will not cover the damages caused in any of the following cases:

- If the driver were under the influence of drugs or alcohol.
- Where the vehicle is driven by a person that the owner did not authorize
- Where the driver does not have driving license

However, in any of these cases, the insurance company shall pay the corresponding indemnity to the injured party, which may be protested against the insurance taker.

Insurance in Spain relating to automobiles can be divided into 2 categories:

- ➤ Third party liability insurance (seguro de terceros o de responsabilidad civil obligatoria)
- ➤ Full comprehensive insurance coverage (Seguro a todo riesgo)

6.4.1. Third party liability insurance

The third party liability insurance (*seguro de terceros o de responsabilidad civil obligatoria*) is mandatory in Spain. It is the minimum insurance required by Spanish law to drive a vehicle in Spain.

It covers the risk for causing personal injury and damage on third party's property (driver and passengers in another car with which it collided, passengers on the car who are not members of the insured family, pedestrians...).

The maximum indemnity this type of insurance covers is:

- ➤ In case of personal injury: € 336,566.78 per victim
- ➤ In case of property damage: € 96,161.94 per victim

In this case the insurer agrees to pay to the insured a stipulated sum in the event of illness or temporary disability, as well as cover the cost of medical assistance.

There are two types of health insurance:

- ➢ Medical assistance: The insurance companies have a wide range of doctors who may assist you. The coverage will depend upon the terms agreed in the policy.
- ➢ The reimbursement of expenses for medical assistance: in this case you choose the doctor, the insurance company shall return the medical expenses to you within certain limits.

The health insurance does not cover some specific situations such as the hospitalization in case of transmissible diseases (AIDS), medical treatment for alcoholism, addiction to drugs, labor accidents …

Frequently the insurance companies do not admit insurances for persons aged over 60 years old, in case they admit them, the policy cost will be increased.

Coverage period is for 1 year, the policy costs are increased every year.

6.4. Automobile Insurance

Many schools in those areas teach most lessons in the local language (Catalan, Basque, etc) and only teach Spanish as a foreign language

International Schools

There are private international schools in most major resort towns, where your child can receive lessons in English. Some of these schools also teach UK exam courses (GCSEs and A Levels) but most use the International Baccalaureate or the Spanish bachilllerato syllabuses.

Price (and quality) varies, but overall private education in Spain is cheaper than in the UK. The National Association of British Schools in Spain is a good place to start looking for international schools.

The National Association of British Schools in Spain (NABSS) was founded in 1978 and represents the interests of some 40 schools, dotted around Spain, mainly in the areas where there are a high number of expatriates. The main aim of the association is to protect the interests of the member schools and those of the parents and children.

The association uses well qualified staff and up-to-date teaching methods. The schools are also popular with Spanish parents for the quality they offer. Further details can be obtained by visiting their website at National Association of British Schools in Spain.

Bilingual Schools

Bilingual schools exist in many Spanish cities and teach the Spanish curriculum, with additional lessons taught by native English speakers. Most of the students in such schools are Spanish and therefore the language will still be an issue you need to think about.

School in Spain is not compulsory until the age of 6, but children generally start school in the autumn of the year in which they turn 3. The legal maximum class size in primary schools is 25, with one teacher and a "floating" classroom assistant who helps out with several classes. There is special provision for children over the age of 6 who don't speak Spanish as a first language.

State School Education

State education is free, but parents must usually pay for school books (which are expensive, although they are provided free in certain cases), school supplies and extra curricular activities. For most Spanish children, school starts with nursery or pre-school at the age of 4 or 5.

At fourteen, the child receives a school leaving certificate. Those with higher marks are able to attend a higher secondary school with less academic pupils moving onto a vocational school.

Enrolling in a Spanish school requires an interview. New arrivals in Spain must have their children's education record verified which can be a long and expensive process. This is called convalidation. A pupil will not be accepted with the necessary paperwork so is best to get this done before arriving in Spain so the child can immediately enter upon arrival in the country.

Enrolment procedures vary from region to region and also from school to school. However for most schools, you will only be guaranteed a place if you enrol in the Spring - usually March or April.

To enrol you must also have:

· proof of convalidation (see above)
· your child's birth certificate or passport, proof of immunization;· proof of residence in the form of a bill in your name. If you haven't got one then a rent receipt, or lease is   acceptable.
· a passport-size photograph (for a student ID card) for a child entering secondary school.

Spanish school hours: These vary from place to place and according to type of school. One typical schedule would run from 09.00 until 17.00 with a two hour break for lunch; another typical schedule would go from 09.00 with no break and finish classes for the day at 14.00. When there is a lunch break of more than hour, students typically have the option to go home for lunch, which many do to take lunch with their entire family.

The British School of Gran Canaria

Is an independent, non-profit making, non-denominational school that provides a complete education for boys and girls of all nationalities from nursery to university entrance.

The education is based on the British model and with the exception of Spanish language and humanities classes, the medium for learning is English. The School and its studies are fully recognised by the Spanish authorities.

Although the School is geared towards providing a British education in an English-speaking environment, it prides itself on being a rich mix of many cultures all of whom unite with ease to form the ethos which is the British School.

The school has two sites. The parent school which caters for children from 2-18 together with the main office is situated between Tafira and Marzagan and enjoys delightful views of the "Pico de Bandama" and adjacent countryside. The South centre, which caters for children from 2-11, is located centrally within the Maspalomas. The pleasant school campuses combined with the high quality of teaching ensure that the pupils work and develop in a warm, happy atmosphere. Each pupil is treated as an individual who is encouraged to achieve their full potential in a caring and supportive environment.

Oakley College

Co-educational nursery and primary school catering to 190 pupils, 3-12 years old, of all nationalities. The school follows the British National Curriculum and prepares children to continue their education in English or Spanish secondary school.

The American School of Las Palmas

ASLP is a private, non-profit, coeducational organization incorporated in the state of Delaware, USA, registered and recognized by the Ministry of Education in Spain.

Pre-School through 12th grade students study a coordinated educational program incorporating the American and Spanish systems, and the most effective international theories and practices of education.

Canterbury School

The Canterbury School is a co-educational day school offering a British style education based on the National Curriculum to children between the ages of 3 and 18.

From the age of six onwards pupils receive instruction in Spanish language, literature, history and geography as stipulated by Spanish law which means that at any moment they may transfer to the Spanish system of education if necessary.

www.ingramcontent.com/pod-product-compliance
Lightning Source LLC
Chambersburg PA
CBHW021053080526
44587CB00010B/239